LUCIANA SAVELLI

LISBON
AND AROUND ABOUT

QUELUZ • CASCAIS • ESTORIL
SINTRA • MAFRA • ÓBIDOS • FÁTIMA

BONECHI EDIZIONI "IL TURISMO"

Importer:
DISTRI CULTURAL - SOCIEDADE DIFUSORA DE CULTURA, LDA.
Rua Vasco da Gama, Nr 4/4A
P-2686-969 Sacavém - Lisboa

Exclusive distributor for Portugal:
ELECTROLIBER, LDA.
Centro e Sul
Rua Vasco da Gama, Nr 4/4A
P-2686-969 Sacavém - Lisboa
Tel: +351-21-9406500
Fax: +351-21-9425214
Norte
Rua da Boavista, Nr 382
P-4415-549 Grijo
Tel: +351-22-7452190
Fax: +351-22-7648620

Revised Edition 2001
Copyright 2000 by Bonechi - Edizioni "Il Turismo" S.r.l.
Via dei Rustici, 5 - 50122 Florence - Italy
Tel. +39-055.239.82.24/25
Fax +39-055.21.63.66
E-mail: barbara@bonechi.com
E-mail: bbonechi@dada.it
http://www.bonechi.com
Publishing manager: Barbara Bonechi
Graphics and layout: Antonio Tassinari
English translation: Studio Comunicare
Photo credits: Archives of the Publishing House taken by Nicola Grifoni
Photos on pages 89 - 90 - 93 - 94 - 98 (*above*) - 99 - 100 - 101: Massimo Listri
Photos on pages 48 - 49 (*center*) - 77 - 111 - 112 - 113 (*above*) - 118 (*below*):
with the kind permission of the INSTITUTO PORTUGUÊS DE MUSEUS - Divisão de Documentação Fotográfico (Pro. No. 260/99)
Photolithography: Bluprint Srl., Florence
Printing: Grafedit Spa., Azzano S. Paolo (Bergamo)
ISBN: 88-7204-463-4

The text in the box "*The Manueline Style*" was
written by Alessandro Listri

Particular thanks to Benedetta Listri, for her invaluable collaboration

* The location of the works given is where they were when the book went to press

LISBON, FROM ITS ORIGINS

There are two legends about the beginnings of Lisbon. The first tells us that the city was founded by a relative of the patriarch Abraham named Elishah; the other, that the city *Olios hippon* was founded by Ulysses, the Greek, during his various adventures, seduced by the beauty of the bay. But it was the Phoenicians, the people of the sea, who built a colony and a large port here around 1200 BC. They called it *Alis Ubbo* (delightful little port) and a flourishing trade soon developed. Lyses was the name used by the Lusitani, a warrior tribe who joined the Celtiberians in fighting the Romans. As Strabo tells us in the 1st century BC. their techniques of feigned retreats and ambushes succeeded in keeping the enemy at bay for over fifty years. Today the Portuguese continue to call themselves Lusitanians, direct descendents of these ancient warriors.

The Romans arrived in Lusitania in 205 BC and called the city Olisippo. It was later renamed *Felicitas Julia* by Julius Caesar, and became a Roman *municipium* and capital. The city prospered under the Romans who beautified it, introduced new crops (such as the vine), built bridges, roads, aqueducts, and left as legacy a language known as Lusitanian Latin, which was eventually transformed into archaic Portuguese. Then the barbarians of the North arrived, the Alani, the Suebi and the Visigoths, who called the city *Olissibona*.

In 719 the city fell under the Moors, from Morocco, and remained under their rule for four hundred years. They renamed it *Al-Usbona*, which in the course of the centuries became *Lissibona, Lixboa*, and finally the *Lisboa* of modern Portuguese.

Under the Moors the city enjoyed an economic renaissance. Palaces, castles, walls were built. The Moors introduced spices - a millenary tradition in the Asian and African Mediterranean countries - brought new crops such as rice and oranges. They installed water mills to grind the wheat. They traded in copper and silver, discovered in the mines around Lisbon. The Moors coined money, introduced the decorative arts of the *Mudéjar* Azulejos and stuccoes. The long Moorish domination was marked by various wars for the *Reconquista* of the city by the Christians, but it was not until October 25, 1147 that Afonso Henriques with a strong Christian army defeated and drove out the "Infidel" Moors, forcing the survivors to live in the *Mouraria*, a quarter near the Alfama.

View of Lisbon with the Sé Catedral and the Tagus River

After the Reconquista, Lisbon became the capital of Portugal in 1255, an honor held up to then by Coimbra, and in 1290 the poet king Dom Dinis I, a lover of letters and art, founded the first university there. João I (King John), the founder of the new dynasty of Avis, and above all his son Henriques known as Henry the Navigator undertook a series of exploratory journeys in search of new lands and riches. With the great geographical discoveries of Vasco da Gama, Bartolomeu Dias and Pedro Álvares Cabral, fifteenth century Portugal lived a magic golden moment with a great empire and territories in all continents. In this century and a half Lisbon became the rich and powerful capital. But it was in the 17th century that Lisbon achieved its economic and cultural zenith with the discovery of gold in the possessions in Brazil. The precious metal flowed into Portugal and filled its treasuries. Sumptuous palaces and castles, and solemn cathedrals, were built to vie with the splendors of neighboring Spain (also engaged in conquering new lands). The original decorative architectural style, known as Manueline after King Manuel I, which was then to dominate in Portugal was created. In the meanwhile Luìs de Camıes, the national poet of Portugal, sang the feats and deeds of the great navigators in his poem, *Os Lusíadas*, or *The Lusiads*, still studied and admired. The imposing Portuguese empire gradually declined.

![The electric tram in Praça do Comércio]

The electric tram in Praça do Comércio

![The futuristic Vasco da Gama tower in the Park of the Nations (Expo)]

The futuristic Vasco da Gama tower in the Park of the Nations (Expo)

One of the reasons was the Spanish dominion over the country, in the middle of the sixteenth century, which, under Philip II, also led to the loss of many colonies in favor of Holland. The coup de gr,ce was inflicted by the terrible earthquake of 1755 which destroyed Lisbon and killed 40,000 inhabitants. The reconstruction of Lisbon was entrusted to Sebastião José de Carvalho e Melo, later proclaimed Marquês de Pombal, minister of King José I. The king himself asked Carvalho to "bury the dead and feed the living". Pombal rebuilt the city in line with a geometric and rational city plan, mirroring the enlightenment which characterized Europe. Lisbon, after the earthquake, never regained its original prestige and power. Proof was the Napoleonic invasion in 1807, repelled only thanks to the help of the English who then remained in Portugal for a long time with strategic alliances. This was also the period in which a new type of music developed among the sailors, beggars and prostitutes and the nostalgically minded in the quarters of the Mouraria, Alfama and Bairro Alto: the fado (*see box*), and the figure of the fadista came into being. A decisive turn in the history of the nation took place in 1910 when Portugal became a Republic, after the assassination in Lisbon of King Carlos and his heir Luís Felipe.
A military coup on May 28, 1926, put an end to the first Republic and nominated Oscar Carmona as president. He

named Antonio de Oliveira Salazar, a young professor of economics in Coimbra, as his minister of finance. Catholic, authoritarian and imperialist, Salazar was named prime minister in 1932 and proclaimed the *Estado Novo* or the New State and installed a Fascist type regime which was to last fifty years. Salazar balanced the economy, adopted an imperialistic policy in the colonies, and succeeded in keeping Portugal neutral in the last world war.

Another coup took place on April 25, 1974, and the Fascist regime came to an end without bloodshed and without a single gunshot, for the women, demonstrating in the square, put red carnations in the gun barrels and on the tanks. It was known as the Revolution of the Carnation and in remembrance April 25th is a national holiday. The many problems of this peripheral country which had lived in isolation for so long surfaced in this new-found

View of the city and Castelo São Jorge from the Elevador de Santa Justa.
Pages 8 and 9: *splendid panorama of Lisbon, the "white city" and the Tagus River*

Democracy, such as decolonization, and the arrival in the capital of a million and more Portuguese from the former colonies (*Retournados*) who are attempting to integrate with the local population.

In 1986 Mario Soares, the historical leader of socialism and an inveterate supporter and promoter of the entry of Portugal into the European Union, was elected president of the Republic. Ever since its entry, Portugal has been engaged in an economic, cultural and commercial rebirth, continuing to be strongly attached to its former colonies. In 1998 Lisbon hosted the *Expo*, the last international fair of the millennium, on the banks of the *Tagus*, whose theme was: *The Ocean, a legacy for the future*.

LISBON, TODAY

Lisbon is magic. Luminous. It is a city that has preserved the charm of things gone by. In no other city is the feel for history and tradition as overpowering as it is here. Lisbon is unique. It is a place of the soul. It is an existential dimension. It is the city of colors and odors; white for the light, blue for the azulejos, pastel tones for the houses, yellow for the sun which at sunset plunges into the water which is no longer a river but is not yet the Ocean. It smells of sardines, cod, cinnamon, coriander, vanilla and nutmeg. A Portuguese proverb says: "E quem nao viu Lisboa, nao viu cosa boa" ("If you haven't seen Lisbon, you haven't seen a beautiful thing").

Lisbon faces the Ocean, but with typically Mediterranean characteristics. It spreads gently out over seven hills, on the right bank of the estuary of the Tagus (Tejo) River in a bay known as *Mar de Palha* (Sea of Straw). Lisbon, as the Portuguese say, is the westernmost capital, the western terminus of the European continent.

For seven hundred years (since 1255) it has been the capital of this small elongated rectangle of a country known as Portugal, no more than 850 km long, but with the oldest frontiers and borders in Europe. It is the capital of a country whose destiny was accomplished on the seas and with its great seafaring voyages of discovery, it built itself an empire, much larger than Portugal itself, held together by a single tongue, Portuguese. Lisbon, with its eight hundred thousand inhabitants (two million in the entire metropolitan area), is the multiethnic city which welcomes refugees from Portugal's former colonies in Africa and Brazil. Politically Europe had forgotten Portugal, but after entering the European Union in 1986, Lisbon became an economic and commercial city, no longer simply the traditional capital of Portugal. Its important port is active again and the city is open and receptive to influences from abroad, while capital from foreign firms flows in, transforming and modifying the economy of the country. Lisbon is a city which has died and been resurrected countless times - from wars, earthquakes, fires and revolutions. It is a city always poised between the past and the future, tradition and modernity, the old and the new, decay and technology.

The only way to truly understand and discover the enigmatic spirit of Lisbon in its various facets and innermost hidden corners is to let yourself be seduced by the city, become part of its life, for this metropolis has much to offer even the most jaded tourist. There is the *Lisboa Antigua* of the fado and saudade, sung in the medieval quarter of the Alfama, or the Bairro Alto, or the Cais do Sodrè, where alleys, lanes and small dark and narrow squares create a labyrinth, where the eléctricos, yellow trams which seem to be saying "I think I can, I think I can" clatter up and down the steep slopes. There is the pleasure-seeking Lisbon by night, which continues on into dawn in the discos, pubs, the clubs and bars in what used to be the warehouses of the port of Alcântara, there is the futurist Lisbon of the enormous *25th of April Bridge* (Ponte 25 de Abril), whose central span is the longest in Europe, over two km of steel suspended seventy meters above the Tagus River, and the Lisbon with its marble and glass structures of the malls of Amoreiras. Or the monumental and geometric Lisbon of the Baixa, entirely rebuilt

Portrait of the Marquês de Pombal

by Pombal after the earthquake of 1755, or the imperial city in its flamboyant Manueline decorations of the Jerónimos Monastery and the tower of Belém which overlook the river and the modern new Cultural Center by the Italian architect Vittorio Gregotti and the immense pavilions of the 1998 Expo, the last World Fair of the millennium dedicated to the Oceans, reproposing Portugal on the European scene. Lisbon is a city that is intrinsically wedded to the Ocean: on it, and thanks to it, trade, commerce, travels, departures, home-comings and landings. And it is from the Ocean that different peoples, ethnic groups and stories arrived, which mingled and were united by the Portuguese language and which gave life to a people that are proud but tend to melancholy and fatalism, polite but not servile, reserved but not sullen (unsociable), bound partly to the past, partly to the future but always proud they are Portuguese, proud of their cuisine, the miradouros, the Manueline style, Camões, Pessoa. Glad they can say, with Pessoa: "*Pertenço à raça dos navegatores e dos creadores di ímperíos*" ("I belong to the race of navigators and creators of empires"). An empire which no longer exists but which made Europe great.

1755: the earth trembled and the city was distroyed

The history of Portugal is marked, one might even say split in two, by the terrible and famous earth and seaquake which destroyed Lisbon in 1755. The earth in Portugal began to tremble at ten in the morning on November 1, 1755, All Saints Day. Three violent shocks, one after the other, accompanied by an enormous roar, struck Lisbon, destroying much of the city.

It was a catastrophe much worse than the Lisbon earthquake of 1531. The city split in two, most of the buildings fell, including the splendid centuries-old royal palace, and more than twenty churches, burying crowds of the faithful who where attending mass on this feast day.

Fire, started by the candles, swiftly spread and a strong wind fueled the flames while suddenly enormous tidal waves from the Tagus River swallowed ships and boats that were loaded with all those who had sought refuge in the sea.

It was an appalling tragedy. When Lisbon counted its dead, there were 40,000. Not only Portugal, but all Europe trembled. The shock waves were felt in Italy, Spain and even in Scandinavia.

But the great earthquake of Lisbon did more than shake the houses, it also shook up the consciences. Catholic opinion in Europe, followed by various secular personalities, tended to interpret the catastrophe as divine punishment on the flourishing and wealthy capital of a country where poverty reigned and which was governed by an anticlerical government. Mutual accusations were launched by the various religious groups: for the Protestants the earthquake was the just punishment of Roman Catholic idolatry, while the Jansenists exulted in the exile imposed on the Jesuits. Still others believed that in the earthquake the Inquisition had atoned for its many sins. The catastrophe also left its mark on the souls of philosophers such as Rousseau and Voltaire, who dedicated several heart rending pages to the earthquake in his famous Candide, *claiming that since there was evil on earth, man was destined to live a sad life.*

The king of Portugal, José I, entrusted the reconstruction of the city to his efficient minister, the future Marquês de Pombal, who "took care of the living and the dead" and designed a completely new, modern city, rigorously laid out and functional as the tourist sees it today: the glowing Pombaline Lisbon of the Baixa and the lovely Praça do Comércio.

LISABONA

View of the Praça Dom Pedro IV from the Elevador de Santa Justa;
below: flower stands on the Rossio

ROSSIO

R*ocio, Rossio* are the fond names used by the Lisboetas for **Praça Dom Pedro IV**. It is the center, the heart of Lisbon, the focal point of the lower city, full of souvenir and craft shops, historical cafés, flower stands, pigeons, where everybody passes by, stops, meets, converses and catches the bus. It is also where the Portuguese from Guinea, Angola, the Cape Verde Islands and Mozambique gather.

In Pombal's 18th century Rossio (the part rebuilt by the Marquês de Pombal), the bronze statue of *Pedro IV*, up high on a marble column, overlooks the large rectangular square with its black and white mosaic pebble paving (limestone and black basalt, the Portuguese *calçada*) and with two splendid Baroque *fountains* of French school. Pedro was a curious sovereign. He was already emperor of Brazil when he was elected king of Portugal in 1826 but he never came there and left the crown to his daughter Maria. Today an affectionate seagull is constantly perched on the bronze head of the monument. At his feet are four female figures: *Temperance, Wisdom, Fortitude* and *Justice*.

Two historical cafés almost face each other across the square: the **Nicola**, once the hangout of intellectuals and artists and the famous ***Pastelaria Suiça***, the pastry shop of kings, where one just has to stop and try the fine traditional sweets.

North of the square is **Teatro Nacional de Dona Maria II**. Neoclassic in style, it was built by the Italian architect Fortunato Lodi in the 1840s on the spot where the Inquisitional Palace stood prior to the earthquake of 1755. The statue of the playwright *Gil Vicente* dominates the facade.

Next to the theater is *Largo São Domingos* with the church of the same name, which leads to the large square *Praça da Figueira* (Fig Square). At n° 8 of the Largo São Domingos, populated by shoe shine boys, venders of roast chestnuts, is one of the oldest and most characteristic locales in Lisbon: **A Ginginha**, where the exquisite cherry brandy produced only in Lisbon is served at all hours.

This Largo, the center of the city, was the set-

The Baroque fountain and the column with the statue of King Pedro IV; below: the traditional locale "A Ginginha"

The splendid neoclassic Teatro Nacional de Dona Maria II in Praça Dom Pedro IV;
below: the eighteenth-century Palácio Foz in Praça dos Restauradores

ting in the far off Easter of 1506, of a massacre during a revolt of the people in which over two thousand Jews and converts were burned. The **Church of São Domingos**, a splendid 18th century building with an interior in pink marble, was rebuilt after the earthquake of 1755 which had left only the high altar and the sacristy standing. Signs of the fire which damaged it in 1959 can still be seen. It was here that the terrible sentences of the Inquisition, located in the neighboring palace, were emitted.

Praça da Figueira, adjacent to the Rossio, is a large very popular square, with small stores, shops selling dried cod, stands and small hotels. In the late 1800s and early 1900s the market was held here daily. At the center is a bronze equestrian statue of *João I* king of Portugal, by the contemporary sculptor Leopoldo de Almeida. The *Castelo de São Jorge* which overlooks the city from on high can be seen on a hill.

Back on the Rossio, on the left of the Teatro Nacional, in *Largo João de Câmara* is the original late 19th century building of the **Estaçao de Rossio**, Lisbon's railroad station, in Manueline style by the architect José Louis Monteiro with an interesting facade with two horse-shoe shaped arches and the statue of *King Sebastião* set between them. From the station one enters another large and central

Facade of the Church of São Domingos;
below: equestrian statue of King João I in Praça da Figuera with the Castelo of São Jorge in the background

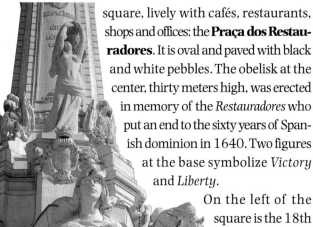

square, lively with cafés, restaurants, shops and offices: the **Praça dos Restauradores**. It is oval and paved with black and white pebbles. The obelisk at the center, thirty meters high, was erected in memory of the *Restauradores* who put an end to the sixty years of Spanish dominion in 1640. Two figures at the base symbolize *Victory* and *Liberty*.

On the left of the square is the 18th century **Palácio Foz**, painted pink, by the Italian architect Francesco Fabri. Today it is the seat of the Ministry for Tourism. A long tree-lined boulevard, the **Avenida da Libertade**, begins in the Praça dos Restauradores. This luxurious monumental perspective connects the city center with the **Praça Marquês de Pombal** (the *Rotunda*, as it is called) and with the *Parque Edoardo VII*, a monumental truly metropolitan vist. This boulevard, part of Pombal's design, brings to mind the Paris Champs Élysées. The Avenida da Libertade is a kilometer and a half long and ninety meters wide. The sidewalks between the central lane and the two side lanes are paved in black and white mosaic patterns and decorated with fountains, flower beds, statues and splendid Art Deco kiosks. What

Praça Marquês de Pombal, known as the "Rotunda"; left: detail of the monument to Pombal

Pombal created here was the *Passeio Público*, to which only the upper bourgeoisie and the aristocracy were admitted through walls and gates. It was not until 1821 that the *Avenida* was turned over to all the Lisboetas.

View of the Avenida da Liberdade in a nineteenth-century lithograph in the Museu da Cidade; on the right: the old Tivoli cinema on the Avenida. Preceding page: Praça dos Restauradores with its pebble mosaic pavement

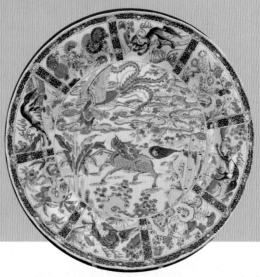

Two important collections of art in the name of Calouste Gulbenkian

The Museu Gulbenkian
(four thousand years of masterpieces)
and the Centro de Arte Moderna

The most important art museum in Lisbon is the Museu Gulbenkian with masterpieces ranging from ancient Egyptian art up to modern times and including paintings, sculpture, furniture and minor arts. This is one of the most important collections of art in Europe, is in the center of the city, and requires at least a whole day to see in the fine premises in which it has recently been installed with the most up to date criteria.

The Museu Gulbenkian is part of the Calouste Gulbenkian Foundation. This wealthy patron of Armenian origins was an oil magnate and devoted himself to collecting art. In the 1930s he even bought many works from the Leningrad Hermitage. When he died in 1955, Gulbenkian left this extraordinary collection to his adopted country, Portugal, which built the Museu Calouste Gulbenkian in 1969. This Maecenas also created the Gulbenkian Foundation which is today one of the richest and most active centers in Portugal in favor of the arts and social initiatives. The Foundation offices are in a modern

Above, from the left: *stone sculptures in the Gulbenkian Park.*

Above: *filigree jewellery by Lalique in gold, enamel and precious stones.*

Left: *Splendid Chinese porcelain vase of the Ch'ing dynasty (1662-1722).*

Below: *Chinese plate of the Ch'ing dynasty (1662-1722).*

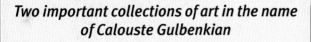

Above, right: *Self-portrait in a group, by José de Almada Negreiros, of 1925.*

Above: *Egyptian bas-relief with the portrait of a pharaoh, Ptolemaic period.*

Below, from the left: *Portrait of a Man, by Anthony Van Dyck* and *Portrait of Hélène Fourment, by Peter Paul Rubens.*

building in the center of Lisbon and include a specialized library and an auditorium. Periodically great cultural events are organized. Both the Gulbenkian Museum and the Modern Art Center are housed in its splendid gardens. The Museum of Modern Art contains works of the 20th century, including the most important collection of Portuguese painters, with works by Amadeo de Souza Cardoso, Almada Negreiros and Maria Helena Viera da Silva.

To return to the Gulbenkian Museum with its over three thousand works, one can begin with the section dedicated to Egyptian art (alabaster vases, female figurines, heads of priests, bronze cats), and continue with the interesting examples of Greek and Roman art, including an important collection of ancient coins. The collection of Near Eastern art includes splendid Islamic carpets, precious Armenian illuminated manuscripts, ceramics and the typical Turkish azulejos. Porcelains, lacquer and jade figurines come from China and Japan. The masterpieces of western painting may be of greater meaning to the visitor. They range from the 14th to the 18th century and include works by Rembrandt, Van Dyck (Portrait of a Man), Rubens (Portrait of Hélène Fourment), Ghirlandaio (the splendid Portrait of a Young Woman). There are also rare and admirable works by La Tour, Turner, Francesco Guardi, the Venetian veduta painter. Of particular beauty are statues by Rodin and the rare and precious collection of jewellery by René Lalique, who was a personal friend of Gulbenkian's.

BAIXA

The Baixa (that is the lower town the poet Fernando Pessoa so loved) on the banks of the Tagus River, located between the Rossio and the famous *Praça do Comércio* is the economic, business and monumental district, the place where the contrasts between the neighboring older quarters, popular and poorer, are most evident. The Baixa was rebuilt by Marquês de Pombal (minister to José I) after the terrible earthquake of 1755 had destroyed half the city and caused forty thousand deaths. In his reconstruction of Baixa, Pombal applied modern concepts and rational geometric town planning criteria. Spacious squares, streets crossing each other in an orderly grid plan, with elegant buildings, all more or less the same height, constructed with anti-sismic material. The large banks, the Stock Exchange and business offices are located there now. The streets, which still have their old names, related to the arts and professions, are lined with shops, some faced in azulejos, high fashion boutiques, music, crafts and large international bookshops. Some of the famous streets of Lisbon are here. *Rua do Ouro* is the street where jewelers and goldsmiths have splendid shop windows filled with objects in filigree of Moorish influence. *Rua dos Sapateiros*, where footwear is sold, still has an old Art Nouveau cinema *Animatógrafo do Rossio*. *Rua Augusta* is perhaps the most famous and busiest. A pedestrian zone, it is paved in mosaics, and is an elegant shopping center with splendid boutiques, bars and outdoor cafés with jugglers, venders of lottery tickets (a national passion) and street artists. While during the day the *ruas* of the Baixa are the liveliest and most crowded in Lisbon, at night, despite the marvelous lighting, they are deserted. In the Baixa everything closes at seven in the evening, and not even the bars, cafés and restaurants stay open after ten. This is the district for trade and commerce, production, and to see Lisbon by night one has to go elsewhere, to the Bairro Alto and the Alcântara.

Recently archaeologists have discovered tunnels and the ruins of ancient Roman baths dating to the first century AD under the network of streets in the Baixa. They can be visited by passing through the Banco Comercial Português. But what gives the Baixa its distinctive air are the *Elevador de Santa Justa* and the *Praça do Comércio*.

The neo-Gothic Elevador de Santa Justa in wrought iron and glass.
Preceding page: Rua Augusta with the Triumphal Arch

The **Elevador de Santa Justa** is a unique neo-Gothic elevator, in wrought iron and glass, with rich filigree decorations, a masterpiece of the late 19th century by the

French Raul Mesnier du Ponsard, a pupil of Eiffel's. This elevator connects the lower city with the Chiado district. Getting on the elevator is like entering an open air museum with its panorama of all of Lisbon, the Tagus and the *Igreja do Carmo*. All of Lisbon, on the other hand, is a splendid city, full of ups and downs, and to move from one level to another without getting out of breath in the lanes or climbing up the many stairs, one uses the elevators and cable cars which every day succeed in overcoming the force of gravity.

A great **Triumphal Arch**, erected in memory of the reconstruction of Lisbon and decorated with allegorical sculptures, such as *Glory, Genius* and *Merit*, leads from *Rua Augusta* into the geometric and monumental **Praça do Comércio**, or *Terreiro do Paço*, the old name for the square. For before the earthquake this is where the *Paço Real* or Royal Palace stood for four hundred years. *Praça do Comércio*, like a great amphitheater facing the river, is a vast square sitting room (a hundred and twelve thousand square meters) with elegant yellow buildings and porticoes (headquarters of the ministries) surrounding the square on three sides. The fourth side is open to the river and a marble staircase with columns, the **Cais das Colunas**, leads down to the *Tagus*. This is where caravels and trading vessels once docked to unload spices, silk, gold, fine woods and fruit from the colonies, and the square swarmed with sailors, buccaneers and merchants. *Cruzados* flowed in rivers,

so much so that to count them faster, a thousand coins were put into boxes of a given size, leading to the Portuguese term *caixa* for a thousand escudos. The caravels and trading vessels have disappeared, but they have been replaced by the passenger boats - a fine occasion for tourists to take a short ride and admire an unforgettable panorama, best if at sunset, from the water. The bronze equestrian statue of *King José I*, by the Portuguese sculptor Joaquim Machado de Castro, stands at the center of the *Praça do Comércio*. On either side of the pedestal are allegorical sculptures of *Fame, Victory*, the royal emblem and the portrait of the *Marquês de Pombal*, minister and man devoted to his king and who left his mark of enlightened absolutism on the period.

It was here in this square in 1908 that King Carlos and the Infante Felipe, heir to the throne, were assassinated on their return from an outing. The second born was wounded and then came to the throne as Manuel II, the last king of the Portuguese monarchy.

On the right corner, between the square and *Rua Augusta*, is the famous café, the old Pastelaira so beloved by the poet Pessoa, the *Café Martinho da Arcada*, which has been making excellent pastries and cakes since 1782. Photographs, texts and a few autobiographic pages are to be found in a room where the poet sat and wrote, in the company of glasses of aguardente. Along *Rua do Arsenal*, on the left side of the square is the **Praça do Municipio**, with a

Two views of the Praça do Comércio with the equestrian statue of José I and the Triumphal Arch.
Preceding page, top to bottom: *view of the Baixa and the Castelo São Jorge from the Elevador and the elevator platform*

Detail of the Triumphal Arch with allegorical statues; on the right: the bronze statue of José I, by the sculptor Machado de Castro

splendid 19th century city hall considered one of the finest buildings in the city with a magnificent inner staircase. The walls and ceilings are covered with a wealth of paintings and frescoes. Of particular interest is one with a portrait of the *Marquês de Pombal* and the *reconstruction of Lisbon*. The Portuguese Republic was proclaimed from the terrace of this town hall in October 1910. At the center of the *Praça do Municipio* is a **pelourinho**, the 18th century stone penitential column with an armillary sphere, the marine symbol of King Manuel I, on the top.

Every city has places and events which best express the spirit and customs of the inhabitants. In Lisbon, for example, this happens in the large **Mercado da Ribeira**, a few blocks from the *Praça do Comércio*, where selling and buying go on daily from four in the morning inside a unique domed building, with azulejos panels, a good cafeteria and restaurant always open, crowded by night owls and revelers who have one more cup of coffee before going to bed after a night on the town. It is here at dawn (which the Portuguese call the *hour of the madrugada*) in the midst of this noisy happy bustle that the variegated humanity of the Lisboetas comes to the fore, a reserved, retiring, melan-

View of the Terreiro do Paço (Praça do Comércio) before the earthquake, azulejo tile outside the Church of Santa Luzia;
below, left: *the Town Hall in Praça do Municipio and the stone column, the pelourinho;* on the right: *stands at the Mercado da Ribeira*

*The facade of the Casa dos Bicos and a detail of the diamond-point ashlars;
below: detail of the portal of the Church of Nossa Senhora da Conceição Velha*

choly, proud, pleasant, available, dignified people.

Continuing our passeio, on the right of the *Praça do Comércio* in the *Rua de Alfandega* is the **Church of Nossa Senhora da Conceição Velha**, with a splendid Manueline portal with an exuberant decoration of animals, marine motifs, angels and flowers. In relief in the tympanum are the Madonna, *Senhora da Misericordia*, King Manuel I, his wife Leonor, Pope Leo X and other figures. The church dates to 1520 and was built on an ancient synagogue, and rebuilt after the earthquake. Inside in a small chapel on the right is the statue of

Nossa Senhora do Restelo, the Madonna of the sailors. Vasco da Gama and his sailors prayed before this image the night before venturing out on the ocean. Behind the church, in the *Rua dos Bacalhoeiros* (cod fishermen) with an abundance of small local restaurants, is the **Casa dos Bicos**, or **Casa dos Diamantes**, so-called after the diamond-point ashlars, with a splendid fascinating facade. It is an old palace dating to the 16th century and belonged to the noble Bras de Albuquerque. It has been restored and now exhibitions, cultural events and meetings are held here.

"I do love the Tagus", says Pessoa

"I do love the Tagus because there is a big city on its banks{....}"
This is what Fernando Pessoa, the most famous of Lisbon's poets, bard of his river

which, in Portuguese, is Rio Tejo. To say Tagus is to say Lisbon. Never has there been a river that is so intimate a part of the city through which it runs.

From the beginning, a profound bond has tied it to Lisbon, which rose on its estuary, fifteen kilometers wide which the Lisboetas affectionately call Mar de Palha. The story and life of Portugal all came from this river and its use, once more intense than now, but which made this city with its trade on the waters the capital of a great empire. The city runs along the river for fifteen kilometers, and the historical memories and commercial activities are concentrated here. The

quays, the port, the numerous piers have been defined by Pessoa "...a nostalgia of stone". The Tagus River, a thousand and seven kilometers long, rises in neighboring Spain, in the Sierra de Albaraccín, to enter Portugal cross through splendid regions where it runs for two hundred and seventy-five kilometers, sixty of which mark the frontier between the two countries, before emptying into the Atlantic Ocean, through a canal known as Corredor, between Lisbon and the peninsula of Setúbal.

Before the construction of the modern Ponte 25 de Abril, which connects the two shores of Lisbon, the passage across the river was entrusted to passenger boats and ferries, still now used above all by commuters. A two hour cruise on the Tagus River is something not to be missed with the feelings the panorama of white Lisbon seen from the water excites. Many wrecks of ships are buried at the bottom of the estuary. The waters of the river, while not as clear as they might be in this stretch, are still full of fish, with sea bream, mullet, sole and sea pike. The lords of the roost here are above all the aquatic birds, such as the stilts, sea partridges, avocets and others, which come to winter here from September to March and the entire area around the estuary between heaven and water becomes a reserve.

ALFAMA

The *Alfama* or Arab *Al-hama* (Hot spring) is the oldest, most picturesque and fascinating quarter of Lisbon which begins at *Rua de Alfândega* (customs street) and climbs up the hill up to the *Castelo de São Jorge*. The Alfama is the place tourists know and like best for this is where they find *Lisboa antigua*. This is the quarter consecrated and celebrated in literature, cinema, the *fado*. Everything there is to say about the Alfama has been said but it is all still told and written anew and memory safeguards that unchanging quality and the spirit which permeates this labyrinthine quarter which, like a kasbah, moves in all directions in the ups and downs of lanes (*becos*) paved with pebbles, tiny alleys, steps, arches, courtyards and small squares. The houses, shouldering each other, deteriorating, with crumbling walls and chipped azulejos and with wrought iron balconies with lazy drowsy cats and birds in cages, are there together with laundry hanging out the window to dry and flowers growing in tin cans. Some of the houses are so close that the sun never makes its way into the lane, and the roofs seem to touch each other as the inhabitants pass each other things from one window to the next. There is practically no vegetation, except for a gaunt tree in the small squares, or for a few glowing fuchsia bougainvilleas and fig tree here and there, growing in the tiny gardens which are actually nothing but narrow gay courtyards.

In the Alfama the lanes smell of sardines, humid plaster, moss, wine, misery and *saudade*. The quarter has dedicated a street, *Rua de Saudade*, to this feeling, so essentially Portuguese. It lies right behind *Sé Catedral*, the cathedral of Lisbon.

The Alfama is one of the poorest quarters, and the people who live there are fishermen, pensioners, artisans and

Below and facing page: *two panoramic views of the picturesque Alfama quarter*

Three fascinating pictures of the Alfama quarter; below: Largo Chafariz de Dentro. Facing page: facade of the Sé Patriarcal, the Cathedral

immigrants and surviving from one day to the next is about all they can manage. But they are gentle people, melancholy and amiable, ready to help the tourist.

The *becos* are overrun with tiny shops selling souvenirs as well as food, taverns, small restaurants and *adegas* (wine cellars) where one can drink a glass of good *vinho tinto* and hear talk of the good old times or what Alfama was like once, in the time of the Moors, with the luxurious buildings, fine houses and mosques inside the Visigoth walls which enclosed the quarter inhabited by the Christians, Mozarabs, Muslims and Jews in the *Rua da Judaria*. The earthquake of 1755 left Alfama almost untouched and projects are now under way for the restoration and reclamation of the entire zone. The Alfama and the quarter of the Bairro Alto are the places to find real Portuguese cuisine, and one canít help but be convivial, time has come to a standstill, especially in the evening when the siren song of a fado singer suddenly begins, accompanying a plate of *arroz de marisco* (rice with seafood) or *cozido à português* (Portuguese style boiled meat).

And if the night in Alfama is full of magic and mystery, the morning is not to be outdone, when the women, the characteristic fish sellers (*varinhas*) extol their fresh fish in the streets and lanes fill with students and young people who come here to eat because it costs less. There is one period, beginning on June 13th (Saint Anthony) the day of the *Festas dos Santos Populares*, when Alfama rediscovers its old reveler party soul and the inhabitants live, dance, sing and cook in the streets, in the midst of brightly colored decorations, fireworks, processions and religious songs.

Automobiles cannot circulate in the narrow streets of Alfama and it is therefore fun to take the Eléctrico, the famous tram number 28, which clatters along the tracks and climbs up the steep twisting little streets to the *Castelo de São Jorge*. For those who have good legs it is preferable to take a pleasantly indolent walk, investigating the lanes and sounds and eavesdropping on the gossip that comes through the windows and doors. Let's start at the bottom, that is from the main square in the quarter, **Largo Chafariz de Dentro**, which takes its name from the *Chafariz fountain*,

which once was inside the walls, and where the *Casa do Fado e da Guitarra Portuguêsa* is to be found. This square is located between the small ***Beco do Mexian***, where the women do their washing in the tubs of a courtyard, and the ***Rua de São Pedro***, a lively lane of small shops and restaurants, parallel to ***Rua de São Miguel***, another celebrated and busy street, also full of shops, staircases and side streets but with a few splendid 16th century houses. The church of the same name is here, with a nave only and a splendid choir, while the altar has a wealth of decorations and gilded intarsias. Not far away is the ***Rua Terreiro do Trigo*** with a monumental fountain, the ***Chafariz d'El-Reî***, in Renaissance style with the Portuguese coat of arms. At this point we have reached the ***Largo da Sé***, with the imposing Cathedral of Lisbon, known as **Sé Patriarcal**, that is the Episcopal Seat, the oldest church in the city. The cathedral, not unlike an imposing fortress in some of its massive walls, is the first Christian monument in Romanesque style. It was built by Afonso Henriques on a mosque in 1150, right after the *Reconquista*. After the earthquakes of 1344 and 1755 it was restored. The facade, framed by two bell towers with crenellations, has an impressive rose window at the center. The interior, a nave and two aisles with nine side chapels, is dark and severe, and the many monuments bear witness to the different periods and styles of the history of the nation. There are many burial monuments with statues and stone coats of arms of the monarchs and court nobles, including that of the *Unknown Princess*, in the many radial chapels, fine examples of the best Portuguese Gothic style, and in the ambulatory. But the Cathedral also bears the signs of later styles, including a few Baroque features. Among the admirable objects is a fine Baroque *crèche*, behind glass, in wood, ceramics and cork by the sculptor Joaquim Machado

Sé Patriarcal - the interior with the rose window and the loggia of the women's gallery

de Castro. In a chapel on the left, with walls completely decorated with azulejos narrating the *life of Saint Francis*, there is a splendid romanesque **Baptismal Font** where it is said that Saint Anthony was baptized in 1195. The *cloisters* around the cathedral are splendid. In the Gothic cloister with two tiers of ogee arcading and sculptured capitals there is a unique Romanesque railing. The *Sacristy* contains the reliquary of Saint Vincent and the **Tesoro da Sé**, a real museum with sacred objects and hangings of great value such as a precious tiara and a *monstrance* (*Custodia da Sé*) in gold and weighing 17 kg, entirely covered with 4120 precious stones, a masterpiece by José Caetano de Carvalho.

Sé Patriarcal - The tomb of the Unknown Princess (1374) and detail of the sarcophagus of Lopo Fernandes Pacheco, 14th century; below: detail of the Baroque crèche in wood, ceramics and cork by Joaquim Machado de Castro

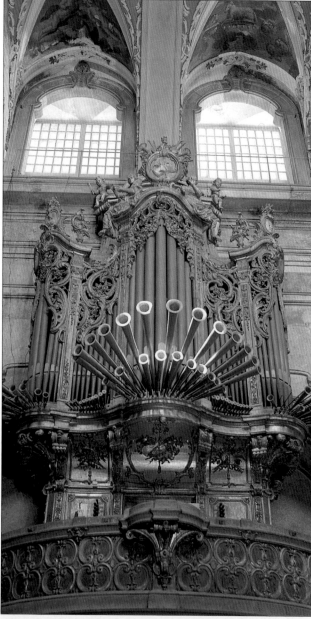

Sé Patriarcal - the baptismal font in the Franciscan cell and the Baroque organ; below, from the left: portable throne (18th cent.), monstrance in gold (8th cent.) and tiara of the Patriarch of Lisbon (18th cent.), in the Cathedral Treasury

Facade of the Church of Santo António da Sé

Fifty meters from the cathedral is the **Church of Santo António**, built on the site of the house where Saint Anthony, or Fernando de Bulhıes who then became a Franciscan friar, was born. He died in Padua and was canonized. White and Baroque, it was rebuilt after the earthquake of 1755 by the architect Vicente de Oliveira, thanks, it is said, to the funds collected by children going from house to house. There is also a museum inside dedicated to Anthony with objects that belonged to the saint, and to the rich traditions that surround him.

Continuing our walk along *Rua Augusto Rosa* and then *Rua S. Martinho Limoneiro*, one arrives at the splendid *Mi-*

radouro de Santa Luzia with its small 18th century church, unfortunately closed, and the *Largo Porta do Sol*, one of the Moorish gates to the city where the *Palácio dos Azuraras* is found. It houses the *Museu-Escola de Artes Decorativas*, with collections of period furniture, silver, gold work and splendid tapestries.

The **Miradouro de Santa Luzia** is one of the finest belvederes over the roofs of Alfama that slope down towards the river *Tejo* and the bay. It is enhanced by a pergola of grape vines and bouganvilleas and benches of polychrome azulejos. Large blue and white panels decorate the exterior of the adjacent **Church of Santa Luzia**, showing *Praça do*

Comércio before the earthquake of 1755, and the expulsion of the Moors from the city. Moving up a bit along *Rua de Santa Cruz do Castelo*, full of typical shops and souvenirs, one reaches the **Castelo de São Jorge**, the famous old fortified citadel of Lisbon, from which one can enjoy one of the most enchanting views of the city, climbing on the bastions if need be. The castle, the citadel and the surrounding walls form a real medieval hamlet, and were the focal point in the times of the Moors. Reorganized after the expulsion of the Moors, the ensemble for a time was the residence of the Portuguese royal family. There are three entrance gates to the entire complex: *Santo An-*

dré, Martim Moniz and *São Jorge*. Inside the citadel there are parks, gardens, ponds with swans and the **Church of Santa Cruz do Castelo**, with the statue of *Saint George*. After the Castle, comes the decadent quarter of **Mouraria**, poor and in some stretches not unlike Alfama. On every corner there are shrines with different images of the *life of Saint Anthony*. This is where the surviving Moors came to live, in a sort of ghetto, after Lisbon had been reconquered and the Infidels driven out by the Christians.

It was here in the Mouraria quarter, in *Rua do Capelão* no. 36, that Maria Severa, one of the first great interpreters of the *fado*, was born in 1846. The beautiful libertine managed a tavern with her mother and evenings sang: *Those who leave, take with them nostalgia. Those who remain feel nostalgia for those who have left..*

The Church of Santa Luzia and *the azulejo tile depicting the saint.* Preceding page: *the splendid Miradouro de Santa Luzia*

The crenellated towers of the Castelo São Jorge and *panorama of the city from the castle.* Facing page: *one of the entrances to the castle*

The Fado and Saudade

It consoles, amuses, intrigues, fascinates, seduces, moves: this is the Fado, destiny, a word that comes from the Latin Fatum: fate.

The song is modular, poignant, composed in free quatrains, a real poem of Portuguese music, the national song.

It celebrates love, passion, jealousy, drama, satire, fate itself and saudade, that mixture of melancholy, malaise, nostalgia for what is past, a word that is impossible to translate. Lisbon has dedicated a street in the Alfama district to saudade.

The Fado, *which first saw the light in the 19th century in Lisbon, in the Alfama, among the sailors, prostitutes and the wretched, later became popular in the cultured and aristocratic circles under the name of Nocturno. In Coimbra, later, among the university students a special kind of Fado spread, more joyous, romantic and ironic sung only by men and still today, in this city, the Fado is only male.*

The story of one of the first and great interpreters of the Fado is legendary. The aristocratic Conde di Vimioso, at the time a leading figure in Lisbon society, fell in love with Maria Severa, a beautiful prostitute of Alfama with a magic and sensual voice. The two had a tormented and passionate love affair that scandalized the conformist milieu. Maria Severa died young and in her memory the fado singers cover their shoulders with a large black shawl. Indeed the fado singers always wear black and are accompanied by the melody of two guitarres: one with twelve cords and the other classic, and the voice, together with the gestures, interprets a mood, which can move

even the most obdurate souls. The Fado has distant roots: in the dances and songs of the African slaves and colonized Brazil, of the Arabs and the gypsies, and the sailors who in the period of discoveries sang to keep homesickness at bay.

Pessoa (the famous Portuguese poet) said that "the Fado is the fatigue of the strong soul".

In Lisbon many clubs and other venues offer the Fado, above all in the historical districts such as Alfama and Bairro Alto, but the ones heard in some dark smoke-filled tavern or on the street are more authentic. Sooner or later someone will suddenly get up and begin to sing and then the tavern and the road become a theater. This is what happens for example in the Largo do Chafariz de Dentro, in the Alfama. Among the most outstanding interpreters of the Fado today are Teresa Siqueira, Carlos do Carmo, Beatriz da Conceiçao, Argentina Santos. Certainly the greatest interpreter of all is Amalia Rodrigues, who recently died, the rainha do fado, for the Portuguese, the great interpreter who took the Fado outside the borders of Portugal and transformed a folk song into an elegant art.

The German film director WimWenders rendered homage to the Lusitao song bringing the beautiful Teresa Salgueiro dei Madredeus on screen in the film "Lisbon Story". In Roberto Faenza's Italian film "Sostiene Pereira", inspired by the novel of the same name by Antonio Tabucchi, the musician Ennio Morricone entrusted the soundtrack to the splendid voice of Dulce Pontes, a young fado singer, rightly considered the heir to Amalia Rodriguez.

GRAÇA

Northeast of the Castelo de São Jorge, this enchanting popular and workers district, with the lovely name of Grace, is distinguished by crowd of panoramic terraces which on most of the houses, between the network of small and large staircases and for two *Miradouros*, the one of *Senhora do Monte* and of *Graça*. The curious **Museu da Marioneta** is located on *Largo de Rodrigues de Freitas*, with stunning panoramas of Lisbon all around. A brief visit to this collection of Portuguese theater and opera marionettes of the 17th and 18th centuries is to be recommended. Nearby is the *Campo de Santa Clara*, a small square with fine 18th century buildings. Every Tuesday and Saturday the bizarre historical ***Feira da Ladra*** (Thieves' market) occupies the square as it has been doing without fail, no matter what the weather, ever since 1882. This flea market is as picturesque as the venders, of all types and races, selling mostly bric-a-brac but where, if luck is with you, you might find something worthwhile, say an African gold coin, old Fado record or some small antique.

The Church and Monastery of São Vicente de Fora

Next to the *Miradouro da Graça* is the **Church of Nossa Senhora da Graça.** the white church, once part of the *Augustinian Convent* built in 1271, and transformed into a barracks after its post-earthquake reconstruction, has a nave only. In the transept there is an evocative wooden statue of Jesus Christ bearing the cross, known as *Senhor dos Passos,* that is Lord of the Passion. The 17th and 18th century azulejos which decorate the **vestibule** and the **sacristy** are splendid.

Moving on down the *Rua da Voz do Operaio* one comes to the monumental **Church** and **Monastery of São Vicente de Fora** (outside the walls), considered one of the finest churches in Lisbon. The fine Renaissance facade

The Feira da Ladra, the flea market in Campo Santa Clara; below: *house faced with nineteenth-century azulejos in the Graça quarter*

has two tiers, with twin bell towers. Statues of *Saints Augustine, Vincent* and *Anthony* are in niches set above the three portals. The church, dedicated to the patron saint of Lisbon, was built (1147) as a result of a vow made to the saint by Afonso Henriques, first king of Portugal - if he succeeded in defeating and driving the Moors from Lisbon, he promised to bring the mortal remains of the saint back into the city. The church was later rebuilt by the Italian architect Filippo Terzi. The solemn interior has a single nave with a barrel vault in white and gray marble, and the Baroque high altar is by the Portuguese artists Venegas and Machado de Castro. Of particular note are the choir and the organ, true 18th century mas-terpieces. Also take a careful look at the **Chapel of Nossa Senhora da Conceição**, in finely worked intarsias and marble. There are also fine 19th century furnishings in the Sacristy. In the **entrance room** to the two **cloisters** there are splendid blue and white azulejos which oddly enough illustrate the secular theme of the fables of La Fontaine.

The ancient monastic **refectory** has been transformed into a *Royal Pantheon* of the Bragança dynasty, and contains the tombs, in black marble, of the royal family, from João IV, who died in 1656, to Manuel II, who died in exile in 1932.

Continuing our *passeio*, leaving *Largo São Vicente de Fora*,

The Renaissance facade of the Church of São Vicente de Fora

São Vicente de Fora - Azulejo tile of 1710 depicting the conquest of Lisbon in 1147, in the entrance room to the cloisters; below: eighteenth-century azulejo with one of La Fontaine's fables, "The Acorn and the Squash". Preceding page: the dome from the inside of the church

São Vicente de Fora - View of the sacristy of the church and *detail of the pietre dure intarsias which face it; below, left: detail of the intarsias of an altar in the church and the entrance room to the cloister*

one reaches the previously mentioned *Campo de Santa Clara*. Overlooking the square is the **Church of Santa Engrácia**, begun in the 17th century but not finished until 1966, with an elegant dome in polychrome marbles that can be seen from all over Lisbon. This church, with its imposing proportions and Baroque style, is known as

São Vicente de Fora - eighteenth-century azulejo with "The Shepherd and the Sea", another of La Fontaine's fables; below: one side of the cloister and one of the bell towers of the church

the **Panteão Nacional** (National Pantheon), for it contains the marble tombs of figures such as Vasco da Gama, Camões, Alfonso de Albuquerque and Henry the Navigator next to the protagonists of modern Portugal such as the president of the Republic Carmona and the writers Almeida Garrett and Guerra Juriqueiro.

The **Church** and **Convent of Madre**

Detail of the Manueline cloister of the Museu do Azulejo;
left: *detail of the portal of the Church of Madre de Deus.*
Preceding page: *the facade of the Church of Santa Engrácia*

de Deus is near the *Estação Santa Apolónia*, the major railroad station in Lisbon. Built in 1509 by the widow of João II, Dona Leonor, the convent was then restructured in the 18th century after the earthquake. The church still has its original Manueline portal, while the Baroque interior is of note for the profusion of elegant blue and white azulejos panels, and the gilded and inlaid wood decoration. There are fine paintings in the *choir* and *sacristy*, especially those depicting the *Torture of Saint Auta*.

The Convent itself houses the important **Museu Nacional do Azulejo** (*see the box Museu do Azulejo*) where a rich collection of painted tiles of all periods is on exhibit. The incredible small inner *cloister* with all its columns, a gem of Manueline architecture, can also be seen.

The Chapel of Santo António in the Church of Madre de Deus

The finest collection of Portugal's most representative artifacts

Museu Nacional do Azulejo

The cloister in the Church of Madre de Deus and *azulejo* panel of the early 16th century; below: *azulejo* panel made in Portugal in oriental style, second half of the 16th century and *azulejo* with View of Lisbon before the earthquake of 1755

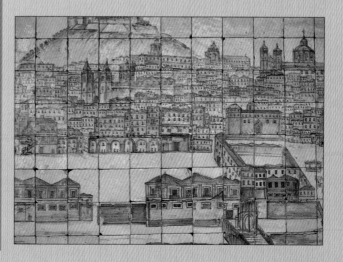

The finest and richest collection of azulejos is to be found in the former Convent of Nossa Senhora de Madre de Deus (Our Lady Mother of God). For centuries these painted tiles have mirrored the art and spirit of Portugal. For further information, see the box in this guidebook, but it can be added here that all you want to know about this traditional art form is to be found in this museum. In addition to countless examples of different kind of azulejos, the oldest of which dates to the 15th century, there is a section dedicated to the techniques. Of particular note and charm is the immense decorative panel in the upper portico of the large cloister. It shows a view of Lisbon before the earthquake of 1755, all done in azulejos and thirty-six meters long.

A lovely 16th century painted mural is also Our Lady of Life, by Marçal de Matos. In addition the museum has a rich collection of twentyeth century azulejos. Before leaving this former convent, donít forget to see the contiguous Church and above all the splendid Baroque **chapel.**

A museum as lively as the city it celebrates

Museu da Cidade

The other museum which is invaluable in helping the visitor understand Lisbon is the Museu da Cidade, in the 18th century **Palácio Pimenta** (Campo Grande). Prints, documents, models trace the history of Lisbon from prehistory to the twentieth century. Of exceptional interest is the large model of the city before the terrible earthquake of 1755 which destroyed so much of it. Rich azulejos panels narrate the life and customs of the Lisboetas. The visit concludes with the famous painting by Almada Negreiros of the national poet Fernando Pessoa, still dear to the Portuguese and the great bard of his native country.

Above, from the top: *eighteenth-century kitchen* and *azulejo panel with scenes of life and customs in Lisbon in the 18th century.*

Left: *The Belém Tower with the ocean still around it, in a painting of 1811 by J.T. Serres*

CHIADO

Located on a slope, Chiado is the district between **Rua do Carmo** in the Baixa and **Rua da Misericordia** in Bairro Alto, and is the crossways between the upper and lower cities, between trade and culture. A terrible fire in 1988 destroyed more than half of the district, and one of the old buildings that was lost was the *Archivio Musicale Valentin do Carvalho*.

Chiado is an aristocratic and elegant quarter, with the most famous pedestrian ruas in Lisbon, such as *Rua Garrett, Rua Serpa Pinto* and *Rua do Alecrin* (at number 95

is the eighteenth century azulejos factory). It is the shopping center, with fine shops, antique shops, historical cafés and old bookstores such as the **Livraria Bertrand** opposite the other famous Art Nouveau café *A Brasileira*, all mirrors, marble, gilding, and boiserie.

Ever since the early 1900s, Chiado has been the favorite spot - almost a shrine - for artists, intellectuals, writers, poets. And today also politicians and the upper bourgeoisie. The odd name of *Chiado* may have been the nickname given to the sixteenth century poet Antonio Ribeira, a former Franciscan friar who lived there. Others say that O Chiado (peasant of the vineyards) was the nickname given to a sly peasant shopkeeper who had a small shop in the quarter. On **Largo do Chiado**, a monument in memory of the poet Antonio Ribeira was erected in 1925. Another, more fa-

The statue of the poet Antonio Ribeira at the center of Largo do Chiado

mous, poet has a curious monument here too: Fernando Pessoa sits, in life-size bronze, at a table in the *Café A Brasileira*, ready to have his photograph taken with the tourists, this man who in life was so shy and reserved. Pessoa spent entire afternoons in this café. He wrote about the Brasileira: "The corners stare at me, The smooth walls really smile at me". **Pessoa's house**, in *Largo São Carlos* at number 4, and now a small museum can be visited. The eléctricos 28 and 15 go to the Chiado but a fine walk is preferable, leaving from *Rua Serpa Pinto*, where the *Museu do Chiado* and the *Teatro São Carlos* are located.

The **Museo do Chiado** in a former 13th century Franciscan convent, is devoted to modern art and has a fine collection of Portuguese drawings, paintings and sculpture of the 19th and 20th centuries. Near the Museum is the fine **Teatro Nacional de São Carlos**, rebuilt in 1792 after its destruction in the earthquake of 1755 on the original site. It was modeled after the San Carlo theater in

Above: *the statue of Fernando Pessoa in the midst of the tables of the café A Brasileira and the Teatro Nacional de São Carlos;* below: *detail of the Art Nouveau sign of the Café A Brasileira*

The Church of Nossa Senhora de Loreto. Above, from the left: *the facade of the church; detail of the sacristy vault, frescoed by Antonio Machado Sapeiro (1714)* and *the lavabo decorated with polychrome azulejos of 1676.* Above: *a print showing the church as it once was, next to the 12th century walls, which are now incorportated and can be seen inside the present sacristy.* Below: *card players in the Largo do Carmo*

Naples, and paid for with the escudos of the Lisboetian businessmen in homage to the queen Carlotta Joaquina de Bourbon. An opera theater, it is one of the finest in the city. The facade is neoclassic and the oval *interior* with five tiers of boxes and seating six hundred is entirely decorated in gilded stuccoes.

Moving up towards Rua do Anchiata at the crossing with *Rua Almeida Garrett*, the main street of the quarter named after the writer, is the old **Igreja dos Mártires** built in 1147 in memory of the martyrs killed during the *Reconquista* of Lisbon.

Rua Garrett leads to *Largo do Chiado* where the gate in Fernando's walls (King Fernando I) once opened, has two churches today, one across from the other: the *Church of Nossa Senhora de Incarnação* and the *Church of Nossa Senhora de Loreto.*

The **Church of Nossa Senhora de Incarnação**, built after the earthquake, has a frescoed ceiling and walls decorated with azulejos panels. The **Church of Nossa Senhora de Loreto**, or as it is called here *Igreja dos italianos*, is the church of the Italian community in Lisbon. Built in 1570 on the walls of the city, destroyed by fire and then rebuilt, destroyed again in the earthquake of 1755, it was rebuilt once more in 1784. The single nave *interior* has a ceiling frescoed with scenes of the *Madonna of Loreto*. The *Sacristy* has splendid furnishings in Pãu Santo wood, a particular Brazilian wood, and blue and white azulejo panels of Flemish design made in Portugal.

On the left of *Largo do Chiado* is a square full of trees: **Praça Luís de Camões**, dedicated to the national poet of Portu-

View of the apse of the Church of Carmo from the Elevador de Santa Justa.
Facing page: *view of the interior of the Church of Carmo, unroofed in the earthquake of 1755*

gal of the sixteenth century, bard of the poem Os Lusíadas (The Children of Lusus) in which he celebrated the discoveries and conquests of his people.

Continuing the walk along *Rua da Misericordia* and turning into *Rua da Trindade* with the **Teatro da Trindade** with a red painted facade, one comes to *Largo do Carmo*, a delightful tree-shaded square with small restaurants, coffee bars and bookstores and a fine eighteenth century fountain at the center, the *Chafariz do Carmo*, decorated with dolphin. This is where the **Convent** and the **Church of Carmo** stand - or better their ruins, one of the most heart-breaking sights in Lisbon, their Gothic arches rising bare against the sky and recalling the tremendous earthquake of 1755 which struck while mass was being said. The *Convent* and the *Church of Carmo*, that is of the Carmelites, were built in 1389 by Gomes Martins, with money given by a general of João I's army, dom Nuno Alvares Pereira, known as the Connestabile, who relinquished all his worldly goods

and became a friar, entering the Convento do Carmo where he died in 1429. The church later beatified him. The *Church of Carmo* was the most prestigious and important Gothic temple in Lisbon.

Parts of the Convent now belong to the armed forces, while restoration is being carried out on the church. The facade still has its splendid portal with six Gothic arches. Thirteen steps lead down into the interior, with a nave separated from the side aisles by superb Gothic arches. They rest on columns with grass and wild flowers growing around the base and stray cats wander around. Surviving panels of white and blue azulejos of the *Via Crucis* still exist in the side chapels. Above the sky is the roof. The *choir*, intact, houses the interesting **Museu Arqueológico do Carmo** with a collection of prehistoric, Roman, pre-Columbian objects and tombs, statues, inscriptions, as well as a splendid 14th century baptismal font and the tomb of *King Fernando I*.

Pessoa and Saramago

While Camões (1525-1580), with his epic poem "The Lusiads", is considered the national poet of Portugal, Fernando Pessoa (1888-1935) is the most original and profound interpreter of the soul of the Portugal of today. His books are in every bookstore, his poems are read and known all over the world, his familiar figure pops up everywhere, including a life-size statue of the poet seated at a table in the Art Nouveau café A Brasileira, in Lisbon.

Pessoa was brilliant, introverted, solitary and highly original. His lived the life of a white-collar worker, sitting all day at a table in a café in Lisbon, writing. What little he published during his life was almost always under heteronyms, literary alter egos (Ricardo Reis, Alvaro de Campos, etc.). This great lyrical-philosopher poet who touched on the great themes of the existence and subtleties of the Portuguese soul in his magic prose, died suddenly in 1935, leaving an imposing amount of unpublished material. Today Pessoa is known throughout the world as the greatest poet of his country. We sugget you read just one of his books: "The Book of Disquiet", considered "the finest diary of our century". A few passages from Pessoa's writing are given below as examples of his evocative style.

Pessoa's Lisbon

"I love the calm and the downtown area during the long afternoons of summer, especially the contrast between that calm and the time when the day again plunges into noise. The Rua do Arsenal, the Rua da Alfandega, the extension of the sad streets that extend east from where Alfandega stops, the entire separate line of silent docks - all that comforts me with sadness, if, on those afternoons, I can insert myself in their solitude".

(From *"The Book of Disquiet"* - translation by Alfred Mac Adam, published by Exact Change)

Mar Portuguez

Ó mar salgado, quanto do teu sal
São lágrimas de Portugal!
Por te cruzarmos, quantas mães choraram,
Quantos filhos em vão rezaram!
Quantas noivas ficaram por casar
Para que fosses nosso, ó mar!

Valeu a pena? Tudo vale a pena
Se a alma não é pequena.
Quem quer passar além da dor.
Deus ao mar o perigo e o abismo deu,
Mas nelle é que espelhou o céu.

(from *"Obras de Fernando Pessoa"* - volume I - published by Lello & Irmão Editores - Oporto 1986)

Quite different in nature and style, but also on his way to being internationally known, is the Portuguese writer José Saramago (1922), of modest origins, who thinks of himself as "more a peasant than a city dweller". He has always been engaged in portraying and recounting the rights of the poor and those who lost out (in their struggles against the latifundium, against poverty). But it was his historical novels such as "Memorial of the Convent" (1982) which brought him worldwide fame and candidature to the Nobel prize for Literature in 1998. An elect representative of the imaginative realism of South American type with sweeping baroque overtones, Saramago's more recent "The Gospel According to Jesus Christ", was considered highly controversial because the sacred figures were seen in the light of a secular and popular piety.

BAIRRO ALTO

Bairro Alto (upper city) is on the hillside. It is the highest quarter of Lisbon with lanes, narrow streets at right angles to each other, and the ruins of houses, clad in azulejos, survivors of the earthquake of 1755. It is the district with a thousand faces, light-hearted, artistic, African, Bohemian, gastronomic and the Mecca of the Fado.

Life here begins at seven in the evening, when work is over, and lasts till after dawn. All this animation and life make Bairro Alto one of the most fascinating and unique places in Lisbon: the mirror of a metropolis which is looking for its place between the past, the present and the future.

Bairro Alto was traditionally the religious quarter governed by the Jesuits, who had their center in the splendid church of *São Roque*. In the 16th century the Jesuits - who were later expelled from Portugal by Pombal in 1759 - laid out the geometric pattern of the entire quarter on the basis of the divisions of the agricultural lands. It is no chance that originally the quarter was called Bairro Alto de São Roque. Subsequently aristocratic and merchant families moved here from Alfama and built their houses. Later the printeries arrived and the editorial offices of the most important newspapers Diario de Noticias, and O Século, and the quarter was rebaptised Bairro Alto of the Journalists. In the **Miradouro de São Pedro de Alcântara**, a splendid terrace overlooking the city with a fantastic panorama, decorated with pool, benches and trees, is the monument to Eduoardo Coeho (1835-1889) founder and director of the daily *Diario de Noticias.* Today shopkeepers, artisans, intellectuals, artists live in Bairro Alto. Young people and students spend a great deal of time here for it is easy to reach on foot from the Chiado, from *Rua do Carmo*, or on

The Elevador de Bica, the characteristic cable car of the quarter and *the entrance to a "tasca", a typical Portuguese tavern*

the old white and yellow cable cars (the **Elevador de Gloria** of 1883, or the **Elevador de Bica** of 1892). Visiting Bairro Alto on board an Elevador is an experience you'll never forget, a small Lisboan adventure that will make you hold your breath, especially when the Elevador passes through streets so narrow it touches the walls of the houses.

There are many fine elegant fashion shops in Bairro Alto: art galleries, antique dealers and jewelers, but there are also old modest shops where everything is sold, from African bread to dried cod to sardine pâté.

Bairro Alto is the place to go if you want to have a good time and eat well, with many discos, music rooms, coffee bars, taverns, tascas, adegas, and small restaurants frequented by the intelligentsia who used to gather in the old historical cafés. One can eat here for a modest sum and listen to real *Fado*, either in the smoky and excellent tavern **Mascote de Atalaia** in *Rua Atalaia* 13 (parallel to Rua Rosa), or in the **Adega Meschita**. The **Cervejaria da Trindade**, in *Rua Trindade* 20, on the other hand is a famous restaurant-pub in an old convent. For a hundred and fifty years the ritual of beer has been celebrated within its walls decorated with old azulejos. It is supposed to be the best beer in Lisbon and it is worth your while to try branca e petra, a mixed beer made here.

A bit more refined is the eighteenth century restaurant **Tavares**, in *Rua da Misericórdia* 37, all mirrors, gilding, stuccoes and crystal chandeliers, symbol of the old opulent Lisbon. Reservations are required and the service at the limited number of tables is impeccable. While eating the skillfully presented tasty dishes, the ear is delighted by the classical music of a string trio of the Gulbenkian Foundation. Time has stopped within these walls.

For those who love wine, a stop at **Solar do Vinho do Porto**, in *Rua São Pedro de Alcântara* 45, opposite the Miradouros, is a must. This bar-wine library is on the first floor of an elegant eighteenth century palace, the Ludwig (Ludovice), named after the architect of the Monastery of Mafra. Surrounded by small armchairs, goblets and transparent crys-

The exterior of the luxurious restaurant Tavares in Rua da Misericórdia

tal up to three hundred types of vinho can be tasted, Port, white, red, young or aged.

Another place to go in Bairro Alto is the unique coffee bar, **Pavilhão Chinês** in *Rua Dom Pedro V*, 89. As if you were in a museum, between five in the afternoon up to two in the morning cakes and sweets can be enjoyed together with fragrant tea, or an excellent Italian coffee, surrounded by collections of old Chinese porcelains, ceramics, art objects in elegant oriental surroundings. The owner, a wealthy charming and unusual collector, after running out of space in his home, has put his fine collections in this coffee bar, offering his customers a taste of a beautiful home together with a fine beverage.

After leaving these premises in Bairro Alto, the real visit to the quarter begins in *Largo Trindade Coelho*, a small square full of antiquarian bookstores with a curious bronze statue dedicated to a vender of lottery tickets (a true national passion) at the center. The square is dominated by the **Church of São Roque**, dedicated to the patron saint of the poor and plague ridden. Candid and imposing, it was commissioned in the 16th century by the powerful Company of Jesus from the Italian architect Filippo Terzi. The facade is modest but the *interior* is magnificent. The single nave has eight side chapels and a wooden ceiling. The marble mosaics and the polychrome azulejos of the 16th and 17th centuries are superb. A profusion of gilded carvings (*talha dourada*, Portuguese art) covers the **Chapel of Senhora da Doutrina** (the first on the right upon entering), with gilded wooden statues of the *Virgin* and her parents, *Saint Joachim* and *Saint Anne*.

The third chapel on the right is dedicated to *São Roque*, also decorated in *talha dourada*, and housing a splendid 16th century painting by Gaspar Dias: the *Apparition of the Angel to Saint Roch*. But the highlight of the church is the Baroque **Chapel of São João Baptista** (the fourth on the left). Commissioned by the extravagant king Dom João V, who spent an exorbitant amount, it was built in Italy between 1742 and 1750 by Nicola Salvi and Luigi Van-

The interior of the elegant bar Pavilhão Chinês and detail of the polychrome intarsias in the Church of São Roque

Church of São Roque - Chapel of São João Baptista, by Luigi Vanvitelli and *an armillary sphere, detail of the mosaic floor of the chapel;*
below: *gilded bronze eighteenth-century candelabra, by Giuseppe Gagliardi of Rome, in the Museu de São Roque*

vitelli, in pietra dura - agates, alabaster, lapis lazuli and amethyst - and decorated with a large quantity of polychrome marbles. It was brought from Rome via ship to Lisbon and reassembled. Pope Benedict XIV consecrated it. The side mosaics of the *Annunciation, Pentecost* and the *Baptism of Jesus Christ* are interesting and can be mistaken for paintings. Spectacular in its size is the great central chandelier with its finely chiseled arms in silver and bronze. The *sacristy* is just as beautiful and rich with a coffered ceiling and 17th and 18th century paintings on the walls. Particularly evocative is the *Passion of Christ* by the Portuguese artist Vieira Lusitano.

Next to the church and not to be missed is the **Museu de São Roque** with a rich collection of religious vestments, work in gold and silver, reliquaries in precious stones, as well as two imposing silver candelabra almost three meters high, weighing three hundred eighty kilos each, the work of the expert Italian craftsman Giuseppe Gagliardi.

After leaving the church and moving towards *Rua da Escola Politécnica* nearby, after passing the **Praça do Principe Real**, one arrives at the fine *Jardim Botánico*, situated on a slope with a fine panorama. It contains many species of tropical plants, from bananas to palms and water lilies.

ESTRELA – SÃO BENTO

West of Bairro Alto is the quarter of São Bento with the **Palácio de São Bento** or **Assembleia Nacional**, the Portuguese Parliament. The palace was an old Benedictine convent, and when the religious orders were disbanded in Portugal, it became the seat of the House of Parliament in 1834. The building with its imposing neoclassic facade has a great staircase in front and can be seen only on permission of the police. Although it is extremely imposing as a whole, the numerous restorations and renovations that were done in the course of the centuries remain visible.

A walk through the ruas around the Parliament can be of interest because they are not part of the normal tourist itinerary. There are shops selling objects for fishing and navigation, carpenter and restoration workshops, small antique and second-hand shops, and many restaurants, taverns and inns, discos and African pubs. You are as likely as not to run into women from Capo Verde with brightly colored garments and turbans, roasting sardinhas and you might even be offered one as homage to the passing tourist.

The Palácio de São Bento, seat of the Parliament; below: facade of the Basilica of the Estrela; left: interior of the dome of the Basilica

Continuing the visit north of the palace of São Bento, the electricos number 28 and 25 take you to the splendid and beautifully cared for *Garden of the Estrela*, with the **Basilica of the Estrela**. This imposing white church is very popular among the Lisboetas, and not only for Sunday mass. Official ceremonies are held here: recently this is where Lisbon gave its last farewell to the greatest fadista in Portugal, Amalia Rodrigues.

The Cathedral was built between 1779 and 1790 by the architects Mateus Vicente de Oliveira and Reinaldo Maneul for the sovereign Maria I, who dedicated it to the Sacred Heart of Jesus, in thanks for the birth of the long desired male heir. Neoclassical, with a facade of two orders, the Basilica has twin *bell towers* with two large clocks, and a dome on top.

The three entrance doors of the church have four columns on which stand symbolic marble statues of *love, gratitude, faith* and *liberty.* Statues of saints are in the niches.

The Baroque *interior*, a nave only, is full of light which filters from the windows of the splendid dome. At the top of the dome is a small terrace from which the panorama of the entire city and the Tagus River (*Tejo*) can be admired. The interior of the church is decorated in polychrome marble, from pink to gray and yellow. On the altar is a fine painting by the Italian Pompeo Batoni and to the right of the transept is the black marble tomb of queen Maria I who ended her days insane in Rio de Janeiro in 1816. In the *sacristy* is a unique Christmas crib with five hundred figures in wood and terracotta, by the sculptor Machado de Castro of the school of Mafra.

Leaving the Basilica and continuing towards *Largo do Rato*, one comes to **Praça da Armoreiras**, near the new malls (the largest in Portugal) all in glass, symbol of the postmodern architecture of new Lisbon, by the architect Tomas Tavira. At Praça da Amoreiras is the eighteenth century *Aqueduto das Águas Livres* (Aqueduct of Free Waters) still in working order, an prime example of engineering and architecture, built in twenty years thanks to a special tax paid by the citizens. The aqueduct runs for eighteen kilometers and has a hundred and nine arches, each sixty-five meters high and twenty-nine wide. At the base of the arches, above the Valle di Alcântara, are decorations with azulejos panels.

A curiosity: the Aqueduto das Águas Livres, built under the reign of João V, had a walk along the top where the Lisboetas used to walk, but which was later declared out of bounds because it was thought to inspire suicides.

Continuing this walk along the final part of *Avenida da Liberdade*, the great Pombaline avenue, we find ourselves in front of one of the finest parks in the city, the **Parque Eduardo VII**, measuring thirty-five thousand square meters.

Lisbon is a city full of gardens and parks, all well cared for, like this one, in the heart of the city, on a slight slope and very similar in style to the French gardens. It was inaugurated in 1902 and named after king Edward VII of England, after his visit to Portugal.

There are two particularly interesting areas in this park with its wealth of hedges and lanes: the *Estufa Fria* (Cold Greenhouse) in which tropical plants, from bamboos to bananas and ferns and particularly fragrant flowers grow in the midst of small brooks, waterfalls, lakes with swans and wooden bridges. The second area, known as *Estufa Quente* (Hot Greenhouse) is smaller but just as interesting: lotus flowers, mulberry trees, cactus, water lilies grow here surrounded by flocks of flamingoes, tropical birds and doves.

The modern glass towers of the Amoreiras mall and the old Aqueduto das Águas Livres.
Facing page: the pavilion for the orchestra in Art Nouveau style in the Garden of the Estrela

View of the Parque Eduardo VII with the Praça Marquês de Pombal and the Avenida da Liberdade in the background;
below: statue in the midst of tropical plants in the cold greenhouse, in the Parque Eduardo VII

Ponte 25 de Abril, the bridge of Liberty

*F*uturistic and gigantic this bridge of modern Lisbon has changed the profile of the city. It is the Lusitanian Golden Gate and is very like the famous bridge in San Francisco.

The 25 Abril, suspended seventy meters above the Tagus River, joins the right bank, from Alc,ntara, with the Outra Banda, the left shore, with the monument to Cristo Rei, facing the river, and the industrial districts of Barreiro, Almada, Cacilhas.

In steel and concrete it is one of the longest bridges in Europe, two kilometers and two hundred seventy-eight meters long, supported by two pylons of a hundred and ninety meters each, a kilometer apart. The central span measures one thousand thirteen meters. The daring technology, together with the elegance of the lines make it the latest monument in Lisbon, more fully an expression of the city and of becoming a characteristic landmark of the urban landscape ñ rather like the Eiffel Tower in Paris.

Built by an American firm in four years, the bridge was inaugurated on August 6, 1966. It was called Ponte de Salazar but after the Revolution of the Carnations of April 25, 1974, it was renamed Ponte 25 de Abril.

Despite its multiple lanes (five lanes for automobiles on the top part, while trains run below), the bridge (toll must be paid on crossing) is always jammed with fast traffic. It is impossible to stop and the car had better not break down.

The view of the bridge of Lisbon even from the window of a taxi is splendid:

looking west of Belém the Ocean can be seen. At sunset, with an enchanting play of reflections, the fiery circle of the sun seems to take refuge under the immense arches of the bridge reflected in the water.

During the Expo, the World Fair of 1998, another bridge was inaugurated, the longest in Europe (seventeen kilometers), the Vasco da Gama. But if you ask a Lisboetan about the cityís bridge, he will talk only about the 25 de Abril.

ALCÂNTARA

At nightfall Lisbon by night comes to life in Alcântara, the port district, which has for some time now become the place to go when you want to have a good time. The discos, the fashionable locales, coffee bars and restaurants of all nationalities occupy what were once warehouses, sheds, offices and customs buildings along the banks of the *Tagus River*.

Night never ends here and crowds of people both young and not so young are constantly on the move, going from one place to the other, waiting for dawn. In summer everyone meets at **Doca 6 de Santo Amaro**, the best place to wait

for the *madrugada*, dawn. Before taking leave of the night, Lisboan revelers go the **Mercado de Ribeira** for just one more cup of coffee and the freshly baked *pasteis*.

In Alcântara you can take your pick of places to go if you love Latin-American cuisine and rhythms, beginning with the nightspot in the **Gare Maritima de Alcântara** with its wonderful murales by the painter Almada Negreiros. Those who want jazz (the real New Orleans stuff) will find it at the **Blu Café**, on the river. Here in front of a revised version of Portuguese cuisine, the customer can listen to the jazz orchestra, surrounded by tall plants, and photographs of American musicians and the old glories of jazz. If African cuisine is more to your liking, you can choose between that of Capo Verde or Angola, or Mozambique, naturally all with ethnic music.

During the day however in Alcântara you might want

Fishing boats in the harbor of Alcântara

to go to *Avenida 24 de Julho* and pay a visit to one of the most important museums, the **Museu Nacional de Arte Antiga**, in a 17th century palace with green windows, known affectionately as **Museu Janelas Verdes**. The old **Convent of São Alberto** is also part of the museum. The museum houses a rich collection of sculpture, paintings, furnishings, precious objects, collections of ceramics and porcelains. Not to be missed in particular is the famous 16th century triptych by the Flemish painter Bosch, with the *Temptations of Saint Anthony*, and the polyptych of the *Veneration of Saint Vincent* by Nuno Gonçalves.

After leaving the museum go to *Largo das Necessidades*, site of the Palácio Real das Necessidades, now seat of the Foreign Ministry. Ever since 1747 there has been a unique obelisk fountain with allegorical figures in front of the palace which was built between 1745 and 1759 for King João V, by Tomas de Sousa as the royal residence which it remained until 1910 when the Republic was proclaimed and King Manuel II went into exile.

The interiors and the furnishings, like those of other Portuguese palaces, were dismantled and offered to the various museums in the city. The two-story palace is painted red and is a fusion of neoclassic and Baroque architecture, with a porch with four columns on the facade. The interiors are closed to the public but the small chapel in which the sovereigns attended mass is open.

The gardens that completely surround the palace with fountains and tropical plants are splendid.

Finally, the walk can continue on the east, in the **Lapa** quarter, seat of the foreign embassies where luxury and style get along well together.

Fountain in the Santo Amaro district; below: bishop and knights, detail of the Saint Vincent retable, by Nuno Gonçalves (Museu Nacional de Arte Antiga); left: detail of the Rococo mask which decorates the fountain in Largo das Necessidades

Fishing boats in the wet dock of Alcântara;
below: square with eighteenth-century fountain on the Rua das Janelas Verdes in the Lapa quarter, seat of the foreign embassies

A collection of classic art not to be missed

Masterpieces of the Museu Nacional de Arte Antiga

The National Museum of Ancient Art is housed in a fine 18th century palace in Ruas das Janelas Verdes. Together with the Museu Gulbenkian it is the most important collection of art in Lisbon. Masterpieces of painting from the 14th to the 20th century are on exhibit here, with some of the finest examples of European and Portuguese art.

First among them is the famous triptych of the Temptations of Saint Anthony, a coruscating and fantastic pictorial narration by Hieronymus Bosch, and then important canvases by Holbein and Van Dyck as well as works of equal importance by Dürer (Saint Jerome), Piero della Francesca and the Della Robbia. Fundamental is the section on Portuguese art which includes the Annunciation by the monk painter Frei Carlos, The Viscount of Santarém and family by the 18th century Antonio de Sequeira and above all the six famous panels by Nuno Gonçalves, the 15th century Portuguese painter, of Flemish influence, who in this work - the only example of his painting that has come down to the present - shows the Portuguese people paying homage to the patron Saint Vincent, in a true kaleidoscope of outstanding documentary interest in a vast and partially mysterious pictorial tale.

The Museu de Arte Antiga also takes the visitor to far distant lands and cultures, thanks to other fine collections. These range from the section on ancient Japan represented, among other things, by the splendid screens of Namban art (southern Japan, influenced in the 16th century by the Portuguese who landed there), the many Chinese porcelains brought to Lisbon in its golden centuries. Among the rarest pieces is a table service of the 18th century, in finely worked silver, incomplete, but used more than once on the royal tables, signed by the famous French goldsmiths Thomas and François Germain, father and son. The great Portuguese power during the colonial period is also witnessed by the many objects of African or Indian origin, such as valuable chests or boxes and tusks, often finely carved or inlaid with mother of pearl.

Portrait of Marianna of Austria, by Diego Rodríguez de Silva y Velázquez; below: Ecce Homo, by a fifteenth-century Portuguese painter

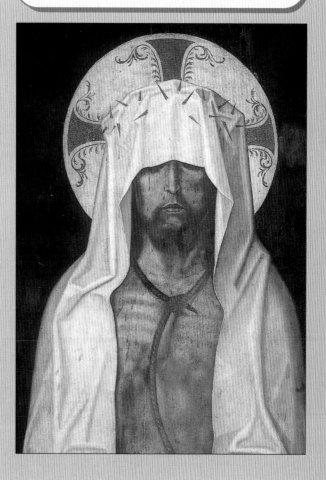

Triptych with the Temptations of Saint Anthony, by Hieronymus Bosch;
Right: *Saint Augustine, by Piero della Francesca;* below: *The Infante,* detail of the polyptych of the Veneration of Saint Vincent, by Nuno Gonçalves;
below, right: *Hell, painting* of Portuguese school, 16th century

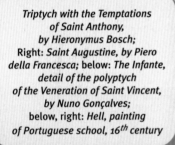

Above: *two details of the triptych of the Temptations of Saint Anthony, by Hieronymus Bosch*

Masterpieces of the Museu Nacional de Arte Antiga

Right: *detail of the Virgin and Child with Saints, by Hans Holbein the Elder (1519);*
below, from the left: *Indo-Portuguese piece of furniture in teak, ebony and ivory (17th cent.); Indo-Portuguese piece of furniture in ebony and ivory, with scenes of the hunt (early 17th cent.); Saint Jerome, by Dürer (1521)*

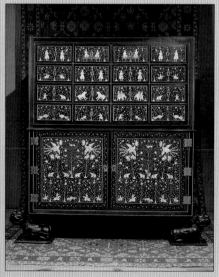

On the other shore of the Tagus
Cristo Rei

The statue of Cristo Rei *(Christ the Redeemer) which looks out over the Tagus River, arms widespread, is tall and imposing. Symbol of the city, it is just like the larger one in Rio de Janeiro. The statue is twenty-eight meters tall and stands on a pedestal eighty-two meters high. It was built in the decade 1949-1959 by the architects Antonio Lino and Francisco Franco with escudos offered by the Portuguese women and collected during the mass held in gratitude for the neutrality in World War II declared by the Salazar government. The Cristo Rei is on the* Outra Banda *(other shore) of the river, in the* **Cacilhas** *quarter, famous and popular among the Lisboetas for its restaurants, and easy to reach by ferry or by crossing the 25 de Abril bridge. In summer a lift takes the visitors up to the terrace near the statue, from which an extraordinary panorama of Lisbon and surroundings is to be had.*

Manueline,
an architectural style

Portugal, like neighboring Spain, enjoyed a siglo de oro, a golden century, thanks to the distinctive Manueline style of architecture and to the azulejos (which lasted one and a half centuries) as well as the enormous wealth gained from the discoveries.

Manueline architecture is a typically Portuguese style. It is named after King Manuel I (1495-1521) who made it the symbol of the empire, demonstrating the magnificence of the Portuguese court to the entire world. Under his glorious reign, which lasted a quarter of a century, many religious and public buildings still visible today were erected in Lisbon, at the time capital of the empire. The Manueline style was the result of a fusion of the rigorous forms of the Gothic (particularly popular in Portugal) and an enthusiastic quest for splendid decoration which contrasted structurally with the empty and load-bearing walls, and with columns and windows overrun with exuberant and fantastic sculptural ornamentation, creating a highly original compositional harmony. This style was then applied to many earlier buildings, resulting in an almost excessive homogeneity.

The Manueline style is a composite of two different souls: one free, imaginative, fantastic, and the other influenced by the various forms of art and architecture assimilated by the Portuguese, albeit with a certain originality, in their journeys and discoveries in Asia (Hindu and Mudéjar) and Europe in contact with the other powers (the Isabellian and the Plateresque of neighboring Spain). The center of irradiation of this innovate style of architecture was the convent of Batalha (1490-1515), in Estremadura, where all the architects who were soon to enrich Portugal with the Manueline style were formed. One of these was Boytac, whose outstanding Manueline structures include the monasteries of Jerónimos and Belém in Lisbon and that of Santa Cruz in Coimbra. Typical elements of this style are the royal escutcheon, the armillary sphere, the cross of the Order of Christ, elements which, together with the anchor chains, algae, ropes recall the ocean and the geographical discoveries, as well as the diet of the sailors and the symbolical emblems of the king.

In honor of Vasco da Gama, the conquistador, Manuel I had the majestic and opulent Mosteiro dos Jerónimos built by Boytac to replace the Marian chapel. Work continued to the end of the 16th century with the imposing cloister built by his successor Castilho. Still today this cloister, together with than of the monastery of Batalha, are ranked as among the most beautiful in the world. The latter was built for Afonso V, but the decoration and magnificence are not on a par with that of Jerónimos.

Another example of Manueline harmony is the tower of Belém. This monument represents the apogee and the end of the pure Manueline ornamentation, by now "polluted" by the artistic-architectural forms of the Italian Renaissance. This stone tower, in the form of a ship, was set to "keep watch" over the port of Lisbon, both as a lighthouse and a control tower.

BELÉM

Belém is the translation into Portuguese of Bethlehem, and it is the monumental quarter of Lisbon. The name comes from a small chapel dedicated to the Madonna of Bethlehem which stood near the old port of Restelo where, according to tradition, Vasco da Gama prayed with his sailors the night of July 7, 1497, before embarking on a search for a new route.

Belém stretches along the banks of the Tagus River where the estuary broadens out and extends out into the Ocean. Near the Alcântara quarter and, five kilometers from the *Praça do Comércio*, Belém is an old district which, like the Alfama, came practically unscathed through the earthquake. Here old picturesque houses, small and brightly colored, stand next to splendid palaces. It is a lively zone, with a wealth of gardens and parks. Discos, coffee bars, restaurants for all pockets are scattered along the river boulevard and in *Rua de Belém* is one of the oldest pastry shops in the city, *Antigua Casa dos Pastéis de Belém*, which has pro-

Compass on the square of the Padrão dos Descobrimientos with the Praça do Império in the background;
below: the monumental complex of the Monastery of Jerónimos

duced custard and cinnamon pastries ever since 1837 and which is decorated with old azulejos inside.

The visit to the monuments of Belém begins with the most important and glorious religious complex in Lisbon, the **Monastery of Jerónimos**, a masterpiece in stone of that marvel of marvels, Manueline art.

Praça do Império with the Monastery of Jerónimos and the Restelo quarter with the stadium in the background; right and below: the dome of the bell tower and view of the Monastery

Monastery of Jerónimos - Detail of the south portal with the Madonna of Bélem; below: *view of the cloister.*
Facing page: *the interior*

Monastery of Jerónimos - Tomb of Luís de Comões; the multi-ribbed Gothic vaulting of the interior; Tomb of Vasco da Gama.
Facing page: the arcade of the cloister

The *Mosteiro dos Jerónimos* or *Hieronymite Monastery* (monks whose task was to comfort the sailors before they began their long journeys) was built for King Manuel I in 1502 on the site of a small chapel consecrated to the Madonna next to an inn where the sailors stayed before embarking. The inn later became a place of retreat for the Knights of the Order of Christ, a powerful and rich congregation which financed various expeditions. Construction was entrusted to the architect Diogo de Boytac and in 1517 to João de Castilho together with the Frenchman Nicolas Chanterène, to end in 1571 with the architects Diogo de Torralva and Jerónimo de Ruão. The entire convent complex, three hundred meters long and a hundred and eighty-nine wide, was paid for by the profits of trade in pepper and other spices with Africa and the East. For a long time, from 1833 (the year the religious orders were abolished in Portugal) to 1940, the entire building was an institute of solidarity for assisting abandoned children of the Pia Casa of Lisbon. The monastery is today a national monument and in 1983 was declared patrimony of the world by UNESCO.

Entrance to the Igreja de Santa Maria de Belém is through two marvelous portals.

The **side portal**, opposite the gardens of *Praça do Império* and the river, is a masterpiece of Manueline art, by Diogo de Boytac and João de Castilho. Above it is a window with buttresses decorated by numerous statues of kings, saints and apostles holding the astrolabe, and it is enriched with pinnacles, sailor's knots, coral plants, armillary spheres, scenes and symbols of the *life of Saint Jerome*. In front of the window is the statue of *Nossa Senhora de Belém* with the *Child Jesus* and, further down, a statue of *Henry the Navigator*. Above the window is a baldachin with an angel with the royal emblem, and further up, at the top, a cross of the *Order of Christ*.

The **western portal** is the work of the French artist Nicolas Chanterène, to the designs of Boytac. Full of niches, arches, cornices, it is also enriched by a profusion of statues of saints which mirror the spirituality of the times. The three central niches contain statues of the *Annunciation*, the *Nativity*, and the *Adoration of the Kings*.

On either side of the entrance are *King Manuel I* and his second wife *Maria of Castille*, kneeling, one before *Saint Jerome* and the other before *Saint John the Baptist*.

The solemn vastness of the space, proportions and sober ornamentation of the **interior** of the **Church of Santa Maria de Belém** are striking and in sharp contrast with the magnificence of the exterior. Six octagonal columns separate the nave from the two side aisles. The columns are decorated with vine tendrils, pomegranates, fruit, flowers and figures from which the Gothic vaulting with its umbrella ribbing springs. Two piers support the

Monastery of Jerónimos - the old Refectory of the Hieronymites

transept which survived the earthquake and the dome is completely decorated with caravels, marine motifs and devices in bronze. The high altar, in Renaissance style, has a fine sixteenth century altarpiece depicting the *Passion of Christ*, an elaborate tabernacle in solid silver of the 18th century and splendid paintings. To the left of the altar are the tombs of *King Manuel I* and the queen *Maria Fernanda* supported by elephants, while on the right are those of *King João III* and the queen *Caterina of Austria*. At the center of the church are the tombs of the princes and of the cardinal king *Dom Henrique II* (he became regent for King Sebastião, who at the time was eight years old). The side chapels are also of interest: that of **Saint Jerome** with a sculpture in glazed terra cotta attributed to Luca della Robbia (others only to the della Robbia school) and that of **Almeida Garrett** with the tombs of the nine children of *King Manuel I*. Opposite this chapel - below the

pulpit of the 18th century organs - are the sarcophagi of *Luis de Camões* and *Vasco da Gama* made in 1894 by the sculptor Costa Mota. There is a small statue of the *Archangel Gabriel* on the tomb of Vasco da Gama and tradition says this is the statue the navigator took with him in his journey to discover the Indies. There are so many royal tombs in the church because the Mosteiro was originally to have been the mausoleum of the dynasty of King Manuel I. The high **choir**, commissioned by the consort of João III, Dona Caterina, dates to 1572 and is in a sober Renaissance style, with paintings on the walls and magnificent benches in fine wood.

The **sacristy**, another example of daring architecture, with a single pier at the center from which the ribbed ceiling springs, contains important paintings.

The **cloister**: art historians are unanimous in considering it one of the finest in the world in its feeling for space, harmony of proportions and ornament. Finished around 1544, the cloister is square in plan, measuring fifty-five meters per side, and is bordered by two superposed galleries with a garden at the center. It is in limestone, and has mullioned openings decorated with small pointed towers. The piers between the two orders are decorated with caravels, armillary spheres, medallions, intertwining plant motifs and strange figures.

At the center of the upper arcade is the plaque dedicated to the poet Fernando Pessoa, while in one corner is a fountain in the shape of a lion, the docile lion we know from the iconography of Saint Jerome. Behind the fountain is the entrance to the *Refectory*, with a ribbed vault ceiling, yellow walls decorated with splendid eighteenth century azulejos. Of particular interest is one showing the distribution of food. On the wall to the right of the entrance is an enormous painting of *Saint Jerome* in the midst of books and with a lion that looks more like a cat asleep at his feet. In the opposite corner of the cloister is the entrance to the *Chapter Hall* with the tombs of illustrious Portuguese including that of the historian and first mayor of Belém Alexandre Herculano (1810-1877).

The **Museu Nacional de Arqueológia e Etnologia** is now housed in the rooms that were once dormitories for the Hieronymite monks. It contains a rich collection of objects from the age of iron, Visigothic gold work, remains of Egyptian, Roman and Arab periods. The jewels, ornaments and coins in the treasure room (*see box Museums*) are also splendid.

On the opposite side of the Monastery, in another wing of the Convent, is the **Museu da Marinha**, where one is immersed in the history of Portugal on the seas with particularly haunting objects including maps, nautical charts and astrolabes and examples of sailing ships, caravels and ships (*see box Museums*). The starry sky, the cosmos and the movement of the stars can be seen in the **Gulbenkian Planetarium** nearby, next to the Museu da Marinha. Across from the Planetarium, next to the monastery in *Rua Calcada do Galvão* is the *Jardim do Ultramar* or *Jardim Agricolo Tropical*. This is a park and arboretum of exotic, tropical and subtropical plants with brooks, bridges, waterfalls, a lake and much sculpture of classical imitation in white marble from Carrara and Estremoz. Tropical birds and splendid peacocks are housed here. An eighteenth century building with azulejos walls in the park is the seat of the **Museu Tropical** with a collection of fifty thousand specimens of plants and over two thousand types of fine wood.

On leaving the Monastery and crossing **Praça do Império**, the garden square with splendid lighting at the center, and heading towards the river, you come to the new modern limestone building, the **Centro Cultural de Belém**, built in 1990 by the Italian architect Vittorio Gregotti and the Portuguese Salgado. Inside are exhibition rooms, a restaurant, coffee bar, an auditorium for

Monastery of Jerónimos - A facade with the entrance to the Museu Nacional de Arqueológia e Etnólogia and the west facade with the entrance to the Museu da Marinha

The Gulbenkian Planetarium; below, from the left: tropical plants in the Jardim do Ultramar and the Centro Cultural de Belém, by Vittorio Gregotti. Facing page: the Belém tower, one of the symbols of the city

music and reading rooms which bear the names of the cities and countries in Asia visited by the sixteenth century Portuguese writer Fernão Mendes Pinto.

Continuing on foot towards the *Tagus River* and crossing *Avenida de Brasilia*, the **Torre de Belém**, symbol of the military and marine power of Portugal, comes into view, solitary and splendid. This Manueline monument was built between 1515-1521 by Manuel I, to stand guard over the harbor of Lisbon and to serve as lighthouse and control tower.

The square stone tower looks somewhat like an enormous raft and is richly decorated and sculptured with pinnacles and small columns, ropes, marine cords, any number of crosses of the Order of Christ, and a royal device of King Manuel I. The Tower, with several floors, has an arched loggia and a terrace on the facade. In a niche, set under a baldachin, is a statue of the *Madonna of the Sailors with the Child and a bunch of grapes*. This is **Nossa Senhora do Bom Sucesso** facing the river. On the first floor of the Tower is the **Royal Hall** and the **Governor's Room**, while on the second there is a **Capela** with decorated ceiling. The Ocean and even Cascais can be seen from the top of the crenellated Tower. Under Spanish domination the Tower of Belém was a prison and was then damaged considerably by the French and thereafter restored.

Moving away from the Tower along the river boulevard *Avenida de Brasilia* (near the interesting **Museu de Arte**

Belém Tower - Detail of the tower and *views of the Tagus River from the loggia and the platform.*
Preceding page: *the loggia and the balustrade with the statue of the Madonna of "Bom Sucesso", or the Madonna of the Sailors*

Popular, a large exhibition of crafts, folklore and traditions of Portugal) is the **Padrão dos Descobrimentos**. This monument was built by Salazar in 1960 for the fifth centennial of the death of Henry the Navigator. It is fifty-two meters high and looks like a caravel about to weigh anchor and is peopled by thirty-two figures with *Henry the Navigator* at their head, holding the model of a three-master. Behind him are the explorers *Vasco da Gama* and *Magellan*, the poet *Camões*, the painter *Nuno Gonçalves*, and *King Manuel I*. Exhibitions of painting sculpture and photography are held inside this vast construction. The Padrão is on a large mosaic space depicting the story of the Portuguese travels and conquests. At the center of the square, a *compass rose*, fifty meters across, is inlaid in marble in the paving.

Leaving the Padrão continue to the **Praça de Albuquerque**, a spacious area with charming red roses and a neo-Manueline column at the center with the statue of the viceroy of the Indies *Afonso de Albuquerque* and four bas-reliefs at the base illustrating his life. Opposite the

Below and facing page: *two pictures of the Padrão dos Descobrimientos, monument erected for the fifth centennial of the death of Henry the Navigator*

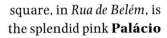

square, in *Rua de Belém*, is the splendid pink **Palácio Real de Belém**, now official residence of the President of the Republic. The Palace is a sixteenth century building that belonged to the Avero counts. In the 1700s it was bought by King João V who modified it almost completely as the royal summer residence.

When the earthquake struck Lisbon in 1755, King José I and his entire family were here in this building and came through unscathed. In 1902 the fine **Museu Nacional dos Coches**, with an exceptional collection of coaches, liveries of the royal house, uniforms and harnesses, was installed in the old stables (built in 1726 by the architect Giacomo Azzolini) of the *Palácio de Belém* or *Palácio Cor de Rosa*, as it is called here.

The *coach of King João V* with particularly rich and opulent decorations carved and painted in gold (*see box Museums*) deserves a close look. At the time gold arrived in rivers from Brazil and the court lived in luxury and magnificence.

Let's continue our walk towards *Calçada da Ajuda*, a steep rua which stops in front of the imposing **Palácio da Ajuda**. This is another eighteenth century palace, never finished, where the royal family lived (1861-1905). The site is splendid and visible from all over the city and it overlooks the *Tejo*. The **Museu Nacional da Ajuda** is here, but some of the rooms are reserved for the President of the Repub-

Detail of the Padrão dos Descobrimentos with the statue of Henry the Navigator; **below:** *the Palácio da Ajuda, seat of the museum of the same name*

lic and official ceremonies and banquets. The palace has a neoclassic facade and three large columned doors, and is full of marble sculpture and fine furnishings inside. Stop here in the ***Hall of Spanish Tapestries***, with the painted ceiling, and with Sévres porcelain and a unique French centerpiece in Empire style by the artist Thomire. The ***Throne Room*** is simpler, with a large Aubusson carpet. The ***Music Room***, with antique instruments, and the ***Room of the Queen***, with the walls covered with blue silk and a bed in gilded wood, are delightful.

On our way down *Calçada da Galvao*, we find the **Igreja da Memória**, a small and elegant church built in 1760 on the site of the attempt on the life of King José I. It is said that the king was hit by a bullet in one arm as he was returning to the palace after a secret tryst with the lady Távira. The Igreja, by the Italian architect Galli Bibbiena, is in gray marble. The mortal remains of Marquês de Pombal often mentioned as the man who rebuilt Lisbon after the earthquake, rest in the small chapel at the side, on the right.

Palácio da Ajuda - The Room of the Spanish Tapestries with a French Empire centerpiece; below: *the Music Room*

Some of the splendid coaches which document
the pomp of the Portuguese court;
below: *general view of the coach room*

Portugal on land and on the sea

Museu des Coches and Museu da Marinha

Extremely popular and perhaps the most spell-binding in all of Portugal is the splendid Museu Nacional des Coches, the Coach Museum, with the richest collection of period coaches in the world, above all those which belonged to the Portuguese monarchy. There are examples from the 17th, 18th and 19th centuries. The most splendid are the royal coaches, those belonging to the church and the leading noble families. The three used by the ambassador Marquês de Fontes when he went to see Pope Clement XI in the early 18th century are stupendous. The Museum also has a fine collection of liveries and uniforms of coach-men and riders.

A glorious nation on the sea, this marvelous, rare and well documented Museu da Marinha is dedicated to the Portuguese navy. Included in its collections are highly evocative pieces. In addition to all that deals with the art and technique of navigation, charts, maps, models, weapons, figureheads, astrolabes, uniforms, the Museum also has life-size examples of vessels of all kinds and all periods, beginning with the papyrus ìshipsî of ancient Egypt. Among the most fascinating pieces, an 18th century brig, the royal cabin of the yacht Amelia on which King Manuel II left for his exile in 1910 and the seaplane Santa Cruz, protagonist of the first trans-Atlantic crossing in 1922. The whole story of Portugal on the seas - including the well documented story of fishing - is here, waiting to be discovered, as the visitor moves through the period of great seafaring voyages and transoceanic discoveries, with real royal barges, warships and caravels. Most splendid of all is the royal two-masted vessel launched at the end of the 18th century, powered by eighty oarsmen and finely decorated in gilded wood.

Prow of a "Moliceiro", typical fishing boat; right: *Naval Battle of Cabo São Vicente*, by Morel Fatio (1842); below: *model of a war and transport vessel, in the time of João II*

Left: *model of a Latin caravel of the type used by Vasco da Gama to reach the Indies and a Portuguese galleon, model of a ship in use up to the end of the 17th century, after the journeys of Vasco da Gama and Pedro Álvares Cabral*

Archaeological splendors in Portuguese land

Museu Nacional de Arqueológia

Founded about a century ago, but transformed a few decades ago, the important Museu Nacional de Arqueológia (National Archaeological Museum) is housed in the splendid Manueline monastery of the Jerónimos in Belém. Included in the collections are finds and artifacts of ethnographical, anthropological and numismatic significance, ranging from evidence from the stone age to the Egyptian civilization (there are also a few mummies), medieval ceramics, objects from the Hispano-Arab cultures, and even objects dating to the 19th century. Of particular note are the finds from the Roman occupation of Portugal including statues, mosaics, everyday objects. The large and fascinating collection of gold work from various periods includes bracelets, necklaces, rings and other pieces.

A room in the museum with Islamic tombstones; left: *stone statue of a Lusitanian warrior and Lusitanian goldwork from the Iron Age in the Room of Goldwork;* below, from the left: *Lusitanian earrings in filigree gold from the Iron Age* and *a stele from Hesemdjet with hieroglyphic inscriptions from the 11th dynasty*

BENFICA

The widely known borough of Benfica is about ten minutes from the center of Lisbon. It is on the other side of Monsanto, a verdant park with pine trees, the lungs of the city. Benfica is the place to go for sport and art. Honors are rendered to sport by the internationally famous soccer team (and the imposing stadium is here in Benfica), and to art by the no less famous **Palácio dos Marquêses de Fronteira** which is an absolute must. The palace, where the noble Fronteira family still resides, is now a foundation which administers the walls and the splendid park, and is therefore only open to the public mornings. The gardens rank among the most important in Europe. The splendid villa dates to the 17th century and is a perfect example of the fusion of architecture and ceramics: azulejos reign uncontested from the palace to the gardens.

The splendid and solemn facade of the Fronteira palace is

Views of the gardens of the Palácio dos Marquêses de Fronteira

completely clad in tiles in a harmonious alternation of floral decorations and statues of historical and mythological personages. Inside, the great rooms are elegantly furnished, with rococo stuccoes, Indo-Portuguese furniture, fine tapestries (note the unique Spanish screen dating to the 17th century). In the *Sala das Batalhas* the wall tiles narrate the story of the 17th century first Marquês de Fronteira Dom João de Mascarenhas, considered a national hero. But the greatest attraction of the site are the gardens, surrounded by boxwood hedges, with flowers and magnificent polychrome azulejos panels. In the *Garden of Venus*, the imposing white marble statue of the goddess looks out over the garden, while mythological statues abound in the other Italian style gardens and the azulejos in the niches depict the symbolic figures of the liberal arts and astronomy.

A splendid loggia known as *Galeria dos Reis* projects over the large basin, completely tied from top to bottom. Statues of the kings of Portugal in white Carrara marble are set in the niches of the loggia.

More views of one of the gardens of the Palácio de Fronteira, considered one of the most important in Europe

A people of navigators and discoverers

*T*he Portuguese ventured out on the Ocean routes in the 15th century, a result of the economic crisis that had hit all of Europe after the closure of the trade routes with the Orient, from which came silk, precious stones, porcelains, fine woods and spices. The period around the year thousand had been favorable, despite various strictures and ups and downs in trade and trade supplies. This equilibrium, precarious as it might be, was broken when the Turks arrived around the 14th century. With a powerful army and an Ottoman empire that had grown in a hundred years, they had first conquered Constantinople, bringing a millenary empire and one of the greatest civilizations in history to an end, and then affirmed themselves in various zones of the Balkans, barring the trade routes between the East and the West. The economy was paralyzed. It was then that a small country on the Ocean, which was already engaged in a war of Reconquista with the Moorish Muslims af-

ter four hundred years of dominion, turned to the Ocean ways, to seek new lands and wealth, thanks to the Moors from whom they had learned what they knew of geography, mathematics and astronomy, as well as navigation techniques. Portugal in those years was governed by a young enlightened far-sighted king, Henriques, known as Henry the Navigator, who changed the course of history in his country, and constructed his policies on explorations, with a great deal of money at his disposal since he administered the property of the Order of Christ. At Sagres he founded a great school of navigation, and the whole nation followed suit, became maritime and entrusted its fate to the sea.

The Portuguese created an immense maritime empire, with Goa in the Indian peninsula as its capital. Missionaries and merchants served as contacts between the East and the West. In the 15th century Lusitania became the most important country for trade with the East, and with a monopoly on spices Lisbon acquired great wealth and became a cosmopolitan capital. It reached its zenith with the discovery of gold in Brazil.

The Portuguese thought of themselves as discoverers and dominators of the oceans, and not as conquistadors, aiming above all at converting the peoples to Christianity. To maintain this immense empire, they were forced to continuously increase their military allotments.

The low population of the country and the inefficient ruling class, composed solely of nobles, led to the political submission of Portugal to Spain and to Holland and England in trade.

Chronology of ocean journeys and conquests

- **1415:** Conquest of Ceuta in Morocco
- **1418-1431:** Conquest of Madeira, Canaries and Azores
- **1433:** Conquest of Guinea and the Cape of Bojador (Gil Eanes)
- **1445:** Bijagós Archipelago, Cape Verde Islands and Sierra Leone
- **1471:** Conquest of Sudan
- **1482:** Conquest of Congo
- **1487:** Circumnavigation of Africa, Bartolomeu Dias doubles the Cape of Good Hope
- **1497-1498:** Vasco da Gama reaches Calcutta and India
- **1500:** Pedro Álvares Cabral discovers Brazil; Gaspar Corte Real arrives in Newfoundland (Canada)
- **1507:** Afonso Albuquerque conquers Ormuz
- **1519:** Afonso Albuquerque conquers Goa
- **1511:** Afonso Albuquerque conquers the Moluccas and Burma
- **1513:** Jorge Álvares conquers Canton
- **1529:** Conquest of Celebes and Borneo
- **1549:** Conquest of Japan
- **1557:** Conquest of Macao

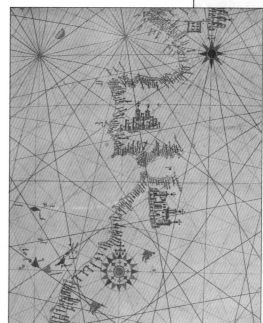

Expo

*T*he first universal exposition of the twentieth century was held in Paris, the last one of this same century was held in Lisbon in 1998 with the theme: The ocean, a legacy for the future. Suddenly Lisbon and Portugal were once more at the center of interest both in Europe and in the world after a long period of isolation that had begun in the 18th century with the terrible earthquake (1755) and which had then continued under the long autarchic and neutralist dictatorship of Salazar.

The Ocean was the leitmotiv of the exposition, and never was there a theme so in harmony with a city that is intrinsically wedded to the Ocean and whose might of old depended on the Ocean - in trade, commerce, journeys, departures, returns and landings. The roots of its culture are to be found in the Descobrimentos.

The last world Fair coincided with another historical date dear to the Lusitanians: the fifth centennial of the discovery by Vasco da Gama of a new route for India. The two events, together, resulted in an imposing project on the shores of the Tejo, on the Doca de Olivais, which revolutionized the aspect of the town. Over an area of sixty hectares in Lisbon technologically advanced pavilions were built to house the conventions, cultural and artistic events of the various countries. The city developed its road and railroad connections and transit system. A new bridge, the **Vasco da Gama**, seventeen kilometers long, was inaugurated in Lisbon together with a panoramic tower of the same name, a hundred and twenty meters high. Portugal spent two hundred billion escudos for the entire work, but it also welcomed twelve million visitors from all over the world and many international artists of the theater, music and cinema who performed in that period.

In addition to the buildings for a new quarter housing twenty thousand persons and known as **Expo Urbe** and the town planning variations, various outstanding permanent structures still bear witness to the imposing series of Expo initiatives. The most striking attraction is the **Pavilhão dos Oceanos**: an aquarium, the largest in Europe and the second in the world, built by the king of aquariums, the American architect Peter Chermayeff, meant not only as a permanent exhibition of fish fauna, but above all aimed at awakening public opinion to the enormous natural resources of the oceans, and the need to protect and conserve them.

The enormous central aquarium and the surrounding four smaller ones are enough to take your breath away. Over twenty-five thousand species of ocean plants and animals live there, from the Atlantic, Indian, Pacific and Artic oceans. The fish in the Pavilhão range from huge sharks to tiny sardines.

Azulejos

There's no corner or street in Portugal which is not enlivened by azulejos, those elegant glazed tiles which decorate so many sumptuous palaces, magnificent gardens, churches, fountains and even benches such as those in the Miradouro of Santa Luzia in Lisbon.

These majolica tiles, original and lively, are one of the most typical art craft expressions in Portugal.

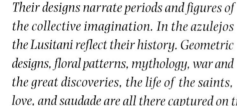

Their designs narrate periods and figures of the collective imagination. In the azulejos the Lusitani reflect their history. Geometric designs, floral patterns, mythology, war and the great discoveries, the life of the saints, love, and saudade are all there captured on tile.

This ancient art goes back to the Moors who had learned it from the Persians and introduced it into Portugal during their rule from the 8th to the 13th century. The name azulejos comes from Al-Zulejg which in Arab means "small smoothed stone", and Azul in Persian and in Portuguese means "azure".

The azulejo became the Portuguese national art and achieved its zenith around the 16th century, after the traditional Arab techniques of Mudéjar *type using the "aresta" and the "corda seca" were abandoned to turn to the technique of smooth majolica invented at the time by the Florentines in Italy. The azulejos where then painted blue and white in imitation of Chinese porcelain, universally acknowledged as the first of its kind. The most elegant and refined period of azulejos is to be found in the splendid noble* **Palácio dos Marquêses de Fronteira** *in Benfica, a suburb of Lisbon, where the azulejos are painted with astronomic, mythological and allegorical depictions. Subsequently, in the 18th century, yellow was added to the blue and white of the azulejos.*

Those who love these splendid decorations must visit the **Museu Nacional do Azulejo in Lisbon**, *in the church and cloisters of the charming* **Convent of Madre de Deus**. *There is an important collection here which narrates the origins and evolution of this unique art and the craft technique. A panoramic view in blue and white of Lisbon before its almost total destruction in the earthquake of 1755 can also be seen in the cloister. The reconstruction of the capital, of which*

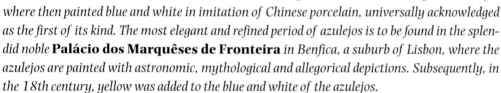

the minister Pombal was one of the leading figures, required the production of an infinite quantity of azulejos, and a simpler style with pastel colors on white ground was therefore adopted. Today the tiles are manufactured on an industrial scale and exported throughout the world, but there are still many workshops where ìmaster craftsmenî produce hand-painted tiles.

Azulejos in new designs or classical patterns are still used today and remain a splendid decoration that is the pride of Portugal.

QUELUZ

The Palácio Nacional seen from the gardens;
below: *the carriage of Queen Maria I of Bragança;*
below: *detail of the gilded intarsias of the ceiling in the Throne Room.*
Facing page: *the Dom Quixote Room, the King's personal chamber*

Queluz, which means "what light", is now a suburb of thirty thousand inhabitants, mostly commuters. The pride of Queluz and the reason for going there is the monumental **Palácio Nacional**, called the Portuguese Versailles by the Lusitanians (Portuguese), above all for the magnificence, beauty and geometry of its gardens. The palace is one of the finest examples of late 18th century Portuguese architecture.

It was begun by Dom Pedro in 1747 and finished sixty years later. It was originally an old manor and was transformed by two famous architects of the time: the Portuguese Vicente de Oliveira, and the Frenchman Jean Baptiste Robillon.

The queen, Maria I of Bragança, made it her fixed residence when the first signs of her mental instability appeared and she left the government in the hands of her son José, after having brought her father's minister, the Marquês de Pombal, to trial. Today the visitor can see the queen's personal coach in the *Corredor das Mangas*.

The Palácio came back to life with King João VI and his young wife, the passionate Spanish queen Carlota Joaquina, who organized Pantagruelian banquets, receptions and magnificent parties with time in between, speaking of the queen of course, for romantic encounters with the young scions, while the king was busy preparing the First Portuguese Constitution and far off Brazil proclaimed its independence.

The Palácio, basically Baroque, has a curious neo-classic facade on two levels and two spacious wings. The splendid *staircase* decorated with stone lions is attributed to the French architect Robillon.

The three sections of the complex are joined by a long corridor, the *Corredor das Mangas*, all in azulejos depicting the seasons and stories of the hunt. The interiors of this palace celebrate the magnificence, the elegance, the opulence of the Court, beginning with the warm gilded boiserie in the personal apartments of the sovereigns. There are considerable amounts of costly furnishings including elegant eighteenth century English and French furniture, immense Portuguese *Arraiolos* rugs, porcelain from China, glittering crystal chandeliers and a profusion of silver and Rococo gilt wood decoration. All this magnificence is even more striking in the magnificent **Throne Room** with frescoes celebrating the royal family on the ceiling and a checkerboard floor in black and white marble. The **Music Room** is completely faced with wainscoting and during the Music Festival concerts and cultural events are held here.

Detail of the painting on mirror in the Toucador da Rainha;
right: *view of the palace gardens*

The **Sala Dom Quixote** is unusual for a circular ceiling which rests on eight columns and is completely frescoed with episodes from the chivalric romance by Cervantes (whence its name) is set over the square ground plan of the room itself. This was the king's personal chamber, and he had access to the apartments of the queen, Carlota Joaquina, through a small painted door. Her apartments included the **bedchamber** and the **toucador da rainha** or dressing room, all delightfully decorated with pastel colored flowers, and large mirrors in gilded frames. One is particularly elegant with a frame of transparent white porcelain. The floor is a masterpiece, in wood in a ray pattern recalling the sunburst of a monstrance.

The *gardens* are superb in style with low beds in geometrical patterns, boxwood hedges, flowers, sculpture, azulejos, water plays, allegorical statues, fountains, basins and brooks all in line with the typical style of the French architect Le Nôtre. There is also an elegant waterfall in the gardens. A large fountain with a circular basin filled with water lilies has pride of place in the *garden of Neptune*, opposite the central facade. A sculptural group of mythological figures, including the majestic and imposing figure of *Neptune*, the god of the oceans, with his trident, rises up out of the fountain.

ESTORIL

A fine promenade (*passeio*) three kilometers long joins Estoril to Cascais, both of which were once fishing villages and have now become fashionable vacation and sport resorts, in particular Estoril.

Located on a plain between the ocean and the tiny "mount" Estoril, 110 meters high (it is twenty-five kilometers from Lisbon), Estoril has developed an elite tourism which keeps apace with the building expansion. Large luxurious hotels, residential quarters, discos, bars, restaurants, elegant tennis courts and a golf course are scattered here and there among eucalyptus trees, palms and cluster pines.

The *racetrack* where Portugal's Formula Uno Grand Prix is run every year is well known. Another international attraction is the *Casino*. One of the largest in Europe, set in the midst of a park, it has plenty of cafés and bars,

The late nineteenth-century neo-Gothic Castle on the beach of Tamariz

restaurants, shops, theaters for performances and concerts.

Estoril is set in the midst of and surrounded by large verdant parks and perfectly kept elegant and geometric gardens with a luxuriant and subtropical vegetation, almost a Portuguese Montecarlo.

Estoril is also known for its *Spa*, with waters that are rich in carbonic acid and are beneficial in curing rheumatism. The spa was discovered and launched by the international nobility in the early 1900s and the luxury hotel, *Hotel Palácio*, at the Spa dates to those years.

There are extensive beaches with fine white sand that are well equipped, but the most famous, a favorite with the VIP, is *Tamariz*.

One of the many gardens around Estoril; below: *view of the famous beach of Tamariz*

CASCAIS

About a hundred years ago, Cascais, originally a picturesque and varicolored hamlet of fishermen on the *Costa do Sol* in the bay at the mouth of the Tagus river, was discovered by the aristocracy and became a popular tourist bathing resort favored by the nobility and even kings. Apartment buildings in cement, luxurious villas on the seaside promenade, large hotels, elegant streets with antique shops and boutiques, restaurants, bars, discos and boulevards with palms - this is the tourist Cascais of today, lively and crowded, and forming the golden triangle of luxury tourism together with Estoril and Sintra. Those who can, come here to pass the winter where the climate is always mild. The beaches are splendid, from the *Praia da Ribeira* enclosed by the bay and overlooked by the Citadel, the *Praia da Duquesa*, with its fine white sand, the *Praia da Rainha*, surrounded by rocky reefs and perhaps the loveliest and most exclusive.

Cascais has the largest **Praça de Touros** in all of Portugal where bull fights are held every week, a typically Spanish spectacle but not quite as bloody and violent here since the bull is never killed and at the end everybody goes home still in one piece.

In the month of June Cascais becomes even more cosmopolitan when numerous artists and musicians arrive for the *Cascais Jazz festival*, an event that has been popular with the public for thirty years.

The ocean-side promenade of Cascais

But the most outstanding sight of Cascais is that offered by nature at the **Boca do Inferno**, or *Mouth of Hell*, the famous rock reef where high waves crash into gigantic caves carved out of the rock by the sea, and exit increased a hundredfold in power and din.

Cascais was elected province by the Romans. In modern times, from about 1870, the Portuguese sovereigns chose it as their summer residence and in the early 1900s the city became the refuge for exiled sovereigns (King Simeon of Bulgaria, Umberto of Savoy) and also a diplomatic observatory in an atmosphere worthy of Agatha Christie. The tangle of streets and lanes, the houses decorated with azulejos and the millenary vivaciousness which each evening is renewed, around the fish, into a noisy and gay market, still survive from the old fishermenís hamlet. Fishermen still go to sea from this coast, with their *traineras*, the picturesque and gaily colored fishing boats with curious eyes painted on the sides to ward off the evil spirit.

Nets for catching octopus; below: *the steep rock cliff of Boca do Inferno*

The beach of Guincho, paradise for surfers; below: *late nineteenth-century picnic basket, in the Museu do Mar*

Activities dependent on the sea are after all still where most of Portugal's wealth comes from. In the **Citadela** are the **Os Paços do Conselho**, that is the town hall completely decorated in azulejos, and the **Igreja Nossa Senhora da Vitória**, a 17th century church also decorated with azulejos. The most important church in the city however is the **Igreja de Nossa Senhora da Assunção**, in Manueline style, with splendid 18th century azulejos of scenes of the *life of the Virgin* and the *Apocalypse*, and precious paintings by the famous Portuguese painter Josefa de Óbidos.

Something else to see in Cascais - the interesting **Museu Biblioteca dos Condes de Castro Guimarães** in a mansion with the *Torre São Sebastião* in the large *Parque Carmona*. The museum contains a wealth of artifacts in gold, silver, ceramics and porcelain as well as sculpture, fine furniture and valuable paintings which belonged to the owners, the Counts of Castro Guimarães. In addition to its collection of twenty-five thousand books, the library also houses archaeological finds. On the opposite part of the park is the **Museu do Mar**, with a collection of models of fishing boats.

In addition to the *Festival of Music*, during the summer months Cascais also offers a succession of dances, concerts and orchestras coming from every part of the globe. In addition, close to the station, it hosts a curious and entertaining *Feira do Artisanato* featuring typical Portuguese products: from gastronomy to wines, from lace to copper and wrought iron, from carpets to ceramics. The artisans work outside in the open air, in front of guests and tourists, who are invited to dance and to taste the good things on offer.

Fresco featuring a nineteenth-century seascape, in the Museu do Mar

A Tourada, *the Portuguese bull fight*

A tourada, *or the Portuguese bull fight, is an art, a sport and a performance to which the Lusitanians are traditionally tied. Engaged in from most ancient times, in the first century BC Strabo already mentioned these peoples who loved to challenge bulls. Around the 12th century the* tourada *was adopted as a useful physical exercise and was taught to the nobles so they could learn to handle their horses.*

It is somewhat like the Spanish bullfight but decidedly less bloody. In the 17th century they stopped killing the bull. New less dangerous rules were adopted after an illustrious nobleman had been gored. Today the bull enters the arena with his horns padded with leather (embolados) *and leaves it still alive. Badly injured bulls are then slaughtered, while the others are ministered to.*

The figure of the Spanish matador *has been replaced by the more elegant* cavaleiro, *dressed in magnificent eighteenth century dress and with a three-pointed plumed hat, who rides a Lusitanian or Arab horse. His horse too is covered with decorated saddle cloths and has tassels in his mane. In memory of the count de Arcos (the nobleman who was killed by a bull) every horseman during the tourada wears a black kerchief around his neck in sign of mourning.*

Throughout Portugal the bullfighting season begins a domingo de Páscoa, *Easter Sunday, and ends in October. In the region of Ribatejo, the cradle of bull fighters and bull farms, where this performance has deep roots, the ancient tradition of bull running in the streets during the holidays is still alive. Crowds of spectators watch the fightes in* Santarém *and* Vila Franca de Xira *or* Cascais. *In Lisbon there are bi-weekly bull fights two hours long (six bulls in every* tourada*) on Thursday evening and Sunday afternoon in the arena of* Campo Pequeno. *The* **Praça de Touros**, *that is the arena, is in red brick and was built in 1892 in neo-Moresque style with four domes with the crescent moon. Nine thousand can be seated and the price of the ticket depends on you are seated:* à sol *(in the sun),* à sol e sombra *(in the sun and in the shade) and* à sombra *(in the shade), and the price gradually goes up.*

The tourada *is opened by music and begins with the* cavaleiro *on horseback already in the arena and waiting for the bull. When the bull enters, he is received by a group of bull fighters on foot* peões de brega, *who provoke and excite him with their red cloaks preparing him for the* cavaleiro. *Now the* cavaleiro *begins a spectacular dance with his horse passing and passing again near the bull, providing proof of his courage, skill and ability. At the end he attacks the bull and sinks his darts* (bandarilhas) *into the animal's back, thus simulating the killing of the animal.*

In what is then called pega, *the final phase, eight sturdy young men* (forcados) *dressed in splendid costumes (knickerbockers, white stockings and short red jackets) move in Indian file towards the bull shouting at him while the excited crowd offers encouragement shouting "Olé". The bull at this point is disoriented.*

The head of the forcados *barehanded courageously grabs the bull by the horns at the risk of being tossed (as often happens). Immediately the other* forcados *immobilize the beast. At the end of this bullfight without bloodshed, a herd of cows and oxen enters the arena, and the disoriented battered bull joins them and all together they leave the arena.*

SINTRA

The hamlet of Sintra and the woods enveloped in fog

Even though Sintra, a small but splendid city of Estremadura, has only twenty thousand inhabitants, it is of considerable historical interest with its old palaces, splendid 19th century villas, lush nature parks, the closeness of the ocean. It is also internationally known for its important annual Music Festival. Wealthy residents and crowds of tourists animate this small jewel.

Sintra lies on the north slopes of the Serra de Sintra and is surrounded by mountains and green hills, with woods, forests and parks filled with luxuriant vegetation and tropical plants. The atmosphere is that of a fairy tale, especially when the mist rises from the ocean and hides the Serra mountain chain and the city seems to be floating. At thirty kilometers from Lisbon, Sintra is considered the "green lung" of the capital. Its happy siting and mild climate have made it a favorite with the nobility and the world of art. Aristocrats still have their villas and sumptuous palaces here. Writers and intellectuals have long elected Sintra as their second home. Among the best known are Camões, Luisa Sigea, Gil Vicente. Byron, the famous English Romantic poet, celebrated its beauty and charm in his "Childe Harold's Pilgrimage", which he wrote here in the place he defined as "the sublime Eden". The Romans, seduced by the amenities of the site, founded the city and called it *Cyntia*, dubbing the surrounding mountains with the name of "mons luna", the mountain of the moon. In the 7th century Sintra fell under Arab dominion and the Moors embellished it with fountains and castles. Today the ruins of the fortress which overlooks the city from on high bear witness to their dominion. It was not until 1147 with Dom Afonso I Henriques that Sintra became part of the Portuguese Kingdom. In the 15th century it became the summer residence of the Portuguese sovereigns, bringing life, verve and elegance to this splendid town where, a few centuries later in 1808, the well known *Convention of Sintra* which sanctioned the expulsion of the French from all of Portugal was signed.

All these features are why in 1995 Sintra was declared "patrimony of humanity" by UNESCO. Despite the masses of tourists and of Lisboans who spend their weekends there, it has maintained, at least in the older part, its uniqueness, the narrow winding streets and lanes lined with low painted houses, and it still has a tranquil and rural life style. The town casts a spell over all those who come to see it.

Sintra is divided into three districts: the old city or *Vila Velha*, with its *Paço Real*, or royal palace, visible even from afar thanks to the two famous conical chimneys of the kitchen with overlook the city. The district of *São Pedro*, in the lower part of Sintra, is almost a town in itself with low white houses. On the second and fourth Sundays of the month a large country fair is held here and just about everything can be bought and sold. And then there is the modern district of *Estefânia*.

The best restaurants in the city at reasonable prices can

Windmill in the environs of Serra de Sintra; below: *the Palácio Nacional*

be found in **São Pedro**, a particularly lively district. These are the excellent *tascas* and *tabernas*, sort of taverns where one can enjoy delicious mixed seafood kebabs and superb soft codfish croquettes, *pastéis* with good crisp homemade bread baked in a wood oven accompanied by the good *vinho tinto da casa* or *Colares*, the wine produced in the town of the same name, in the neighboring hills, better if seven years old. Lastly a delight to the palate are the exquisite queijadas, famous tarts made with cheese, almonds and cinnamon, a specialty of Sintra ever since the 13th century.

Estefânia, the third district, is the modern part of the city, near the station. It is the part where hotels, craft and souvenir shops are to be found, as well as the fine municipal *Parque da Libertade*.

Palácio Nacional - the Sala dos Árabes; below: *detail of the dome of the Sala dos Brasões (of the Coats of Arms).*
Facing page: *the Sala dos Brasões*

Sintra, which aspires to become the cultural capital of modern Portugal, every hear hosts important events, conventions and international encounters. The most important happening in the city is from June to September when Sintra opens its palaces and mansions to welcome the by now famous *International Music Festival* (classic, chamber, jazz and opera) and organizes legendary historical reconstructions which attract an international public. On June 29th the city celebrates its patron saint, São Pedro, with a traditional large fair which attracts merchants, vendors and peddlers from all over Portugal and the city sings and dances in the streets.

The **Paço Real**, or **Palácio Nacional**, is a true Portuguese Alhambra overlooking the city. It stands in the historical center and witnessed the most significant moments of Portugal's history, such as the birth and fall of the empire. The Palace, originally Moorish in its structure, was enlarged and modified by João I at the beginning of the 15th century, who enhanced the interiors with splendid *Mudéjar azulejos* (glazed tiles). Today it has the most important collection of azulejos in the world .

The mixture of Moorish, Gothic, Manueline and Renaissance styles in the Palace has made it incredibly unique and fascinating and it is considered the pearl and symbol of Sintra. In the *Sala dos Árabes*, one of the marvels of the palace, in pure Moorish style, with a marble fountain at the center, the walls are a mosaic of marvelous 15th and 16th century azulejos. These glazed tiles, together with the exuberant Manueline style, are the most original and vivid expression of Portuguese art.

One of the oldest rooms is the *Sala dos Brasões* or *Room of the Coats of Arms*, with a precious octagonal domed ceiling in carved wood, completely painted with the coats of arms of the seventy-two noble families of Portugal. At the center of the dome is the crest of King Manuel (whence the name of the Manueline style) and his eight children. The walls of the room are covered with blue and white azulejos painted with pictures of the hunt and of war. On the floor is an excellently preserved splendid Persian rug. Next to this room is the small bedchamber where, it is said, King Afonso VI was kept a prisoner by his brother Pedro for nine long years (until his death in 1683) considered incapable of governing because he was mentally deranged. Pedro took over the throne and when he became King Pedro II, he also married the wife of his unfortunate brother, the Italian princess Marie Françoise Elisabeth of Savoy-Nemours.

The Palácio Nacional da Pena

One of the largest room in the palace is the **Sala dos Cisnes** (Room of the Swans), so-called because of the twenty-seven white swans which elegantly decorate the wooden ceiling. Here sumptuous banquets were held in the presence of the king.

The charming **Sala das Pegas**, or Room of the Magpies, is named after the one hundred and thirty-six magpies painted over the entire ceiling, bearing in their beaks a ribbon with written on it *"por bem"*, for a good purpose. Tradition says that these one hundred and thirty-six mag-

pies, as many as the women in the court, were painted on commission from Dom João I, a great Don Juan who was irritated by the constant chattering of so many women, and had them wittily represented as magpies. The king was caught by his wife Philippa of Lancaster, whom he married as a result of the treaty of Windsor, kissing and flirting with a lady-in-waiting. Filled with consternation, he is said to have exclaimed, almost as an excuse, the phrase*"por bem"*.

Before leaving the royal palace take a good look not only

at the chapel with its wealth of splendid azulejos, built by João on the site of an old mosque, but also the palace gardens, with patios and courtyards, oases overflowing with fragrant flowers and exotic plants, climbing jasmine, white carpets of lily of the valley, rhododendron, camellias, myrtle, water lilies, rows of orange and lemon trees, figs, pepper trees, a profusion of basins and fountains ‹ ing with water.

The **Castelo dos Mouros**, the old‹ ument of Sintra, clings to two pe‹ Serra, only three kilometers fro‹ cio. Little remains of this mill‹ splendid views can be had fr‹ over the ocean at sunset i‹ magical.

The *Castelo*, originally a to‹ around the 8th century. The walls w‹ towers wind around and embrace the mo‹

The *Castelo dos Mouros* was conquered in 1147, after many attempts, by Afonso Henriques, who had a strong Christian army and drove out all the Moors. This was when the first Christian chapel in the entire region was built, dedicated to São Pedro de Penaferrim. In the Romantic period, in 1860, it was restored on commission of King Fernando II. Inside the castle the *Cisterna Moura* and the *Torreão Real* (Royal Tower) can still be seen.

The most original and scenic construction stands on the top of the hill of Sintra. The **Palácio Nacional da Pena** was built by Fer‹ ‹ Saxe-Coburg-Gotha on the ruins of ‹ monastery of the 16th cen‹ ‹ made of the exquis‹ ‹ lácio. The two ‹ r over

Palácio Nacional da Pena - Detail o‹

Palácio Nacional da Pena - Two pictures of the Chapel of Nossa Senhora da Pena: altarpiece in marble and alabaster and detail of the ceiling with its Gothic Manueline ribbing; below: the Indian Room

swans and other aquatic animals. A charming lodge, hidden among the trees, can be visited. It was built by Ferdinand for his "lady love", the countess of Edla, a famous opera singer of the time. Richard Strauss was also a guest at the palace.

The mixture of styles - Gothic towers, Moorish minarets, Manueline and Renaissance architecture, and even Baroque and Bavarian - is the work of an eccentric and imaginative Bavarian architect, Baron von Eschwege. The queen Maria II and her husband Ferdinand of Saxe-Coburg-Gotha had asked him to build a romantic castle for their summer sojourns.

Inside the *Palácio*, the richly furnished rooms include splendid paintings, collections of ceramics, fine porcelains. Ceilings and walls are frescoed, and unique is the **Sala dos Nus** (Room of the Nudes) or *Atelier*, with frescoes of appropriate subject. Nothing has been touch since 1910 when the sovereigns abandoned Portugal because of the revolution. The *Arraiolos* carpets of Portuguese manufacture are noteworthy, but their technique was that of the Arabs: hand made multicolored carpets with floral patterns, palms, animals, so dear to the English who bought many to embellish their homes.

The remains of the *Chapel* and *Cloister* in this palace are of particular interest. On the altar in the *Capela de Nossa Senhora da Pena* - which belonged to the original Hieronymite monastery - is a well preserved splendid Renaissance panel (*retablo*) with elaborate inlays in black marble and alabaster, by the French 16th century sculptor Nicolas Chanterène.

The old *Cloister* with its elegant cross vaulting, is built on two levels in Manueline stile and the walls are faced with azulejos.

Another jewel of Sintra is the secluded **Convento dos Capuchos** (now closed) known also as "**de Santa Cruz**" or "**da Cortiça**" or Cork Convent. The austere bare monastery stands in the rocks, in dense silent woods, where the only sounds to be heard are the occasional twittering of the birds. It was built in 1160 by Alvaro de Castro to fulfil a vow made by his father João de Castro, viceroy of India.

The monastery inside is a labyrinth of narrow corridors, chapels and cells curiously all lined with cork. *Cortiça* or cork may have been used so as to keep out the humidity or to favor the acoustic isolation required for the meditation of the friars who lived there until 1938 when the monastery became a museum.

Next to its museums and palaces, Sintra also has splendid private villas or estates of the nobility, known as *Quintas*, but unfortunately only a few can be visited. Among the most interesting is the 18th-19th century *Quinta de Monserrate*, not far from the historical center, but now abandoned. The park is outstanding and all kinds and colors of roses are grown in an area of thirty hectares.

A splendid villa, now transformed into a luxury hotel, is

Azenhas do Mar, detail of a public fountain at the entrance to the town; below: view of the hamlet with a sheer drop to the sea

Cabo da Roca, the westernmost promontory of Europe

the *Quinta de Seteais* (Palace of Sighs), on the outskirts of the city built by the Dutch consul Daniel Gildmeester in the 18th century.

Various excursions can be made into the surroundings of Sintra. One of these is towards the ocean, passing through **Azenhas do Mar**, a delightful hamlet of fishermen which smells of grilled *sardinhas* and with white houses with colored windows peering out of the cliffs that drop sheer to the sea. The picturesque panorama that greets the eye where Azenhas do Mar overlooks the gulf is the work of the sea, which eroded the rocks to form natural pools.

Continuing the excursion towards the Atlantic, the next stop is **Cabo da Roca**. The Tourist Office here will give all visitors (upon payment of a few escudos) an artistic certificate which attests to the fact that they have passed through the furthermost point of the old continent.

Indeed Cabo da Roca is the westernmost promontory of Europe (known by the ancient Romans as *Promontorium Magnum*), a fascinating and wind swept cliff that drops a hundred and forty meters to the sea. It is the last strip of land, and an epigraph by the poet Camões to be found here says: "Here where the land ends, the unknown begins". The old lighthouse on the cape has been functioning since 1772, and was electrified in 1932. A stone cross set high on a column overlooks it all.

The Wines

King of all the wines of Portugal is undoubtedly the legendary **Port**, produced in the region of the Douro, matured - by law - in the cellars in the zone of Vila Nova da Gaia nearby. There are different kinds - as will be explained further on - but whichever one you choose, the wine must always be poured from a pitcher. It was apparently first created in the early 1900s, thanks to the agronomic-commercial collaboration between the English and the Portuguese, and is now one of the finest wines in the world and exported to all continents. The authoritative Instituto do Vino do Porto (Port Wine Institute) supervises the vineyards in the Alto Douro area, where there are various types of grapes, and rigorously controls every step in the long process required before the wine ends up on some lucky table. Grown under the supervision of expert agronomists in the numerous quintas, large and enchanting white farms, after its fermentation it is taken to Villa Nova de Gaia in barrels where it remains for years to mature. Every bottle, at the end, must bear the selo de origem, a distinctive mark which testifies to its origin and quality. At the vertex of Port is the so-called Vintage Port, as famous as it is expensive, obtained from grapes of a single vintage year defined by the experts as a golden year. For example 1963, 1977, 1985 were golden years. Years are required for its maturation and it is considered excellent after ten, but supreme after fifteen or twenty years. Another equally famous but not quite as exclusive quality is "Porto with delayed bottling". One more in this list is the so-called "Port aged in wood", the result of a mixture of different vintage years aged in oak barrels. So much has been written about Port, as about all legendary wines, endowed with a rich symbolism and precise rituals, which includes tasting, which the traveler can learn by visiting the areas of production in Portugal and the great wine cellars.

But Port is not the only Portuguese wine. The country produces many other excellent wines including the well known and appreciated vinhos verdes, which come from the zone of Minho, south-western territory of Portugal. Vine growing has ancient traditions here and employs almost two hundred thousand people. **Vinho verde** can be white (blanco) or red (tinto), and is a light slightly sparkling wine of never more than eleven percent alcoholic content and will vary according to the six zones of origin and production. This wine too is protected and guaranteed by an "Association of producers and bottlers of vinho verde".

Good Portuguese wines also come from various other regions such as Bairrada, near Coimbra, which makes an excellent red, or Douro itself which produces other wines in addition to the famous Port. The excellent **blanco de Bucelas** comes from around Lisbon while other no less interesting wines come from Colares near Sintra, and from Algarve, in the south. Lastly the **vinho de Madeira** is one of the oldest and most highly appreciated of Portugal's famous sweet wines.

MAFRA

Mafra with its eight thousand inhabitants is located on a green plain ten kilometers from the Atlantic and forty kilometers from Lisbon. It is a pleasant rustic town which lives on agriculture, tourism and crafts, with pretty streets and an orderly life style characterized by peaceful old farm customs. The inhabitants are hospitable, friendly and deeply religious. The most significant and extraordinary religious event in Mafra, in which the entire population takes part, is the *procession of the Terceiros* on the fourth Sunday of Lent and which attracts many tourists. The procession also includes carriages decorated with old religious hangings donated by Dom João in the 18th century. This religious festival is also cheered by a delicious and traditional Easter cake, the *Paõ doce*, skillfully and fervidly prepared by the local women.

The most important building of Mafra is the **Mosteiro-Palácio**, at the center of the town and so imposing it can be seen from everywhere. It stretches out over four hectares and in addition to a monastery consists of a *Basilica*, the *royal palace* and the *convent buildings*. It is square in plan, with the main facade in marble and two large square towers with onion domes at the sides. The Baroque facade of the Basilica is also flanked by two bell towers.

João V had this complex built on an old Capuchin monastery in gratitude for the birth of a long awaited heir. The **Palace** was built between 1717 and 1730 by the German Friedrich Ludwig (Ludovice as he liked to be called) and was paid for with the gold which flowed in from the rich mines in Brazil. The ambitious and extravagant king intended it to compete in magnificence and grandeur with the greatest Spanish palaces. It is no coincidence that the *Mosteiro-Palácio* is called the *Portuguese Escorial*. Portuguese historians maintain that, because he was the most magnificent, Joao V was the last of the kings of Portugal.

The immense palace has nine hundred finely furnished rooms, and doorways and windows together number more than four thousand. The Portuguese economy and wealth was at its zenith, and more than forty thousand laborers, sculptors and artists were employed on the palace. Many of them were Italian. A thousand oxen brought in the

Palácio Nacional de Mafra - the Hall of the Hunt in the royal apartments; below: statue of Saint Francis of Paola (18th cent.)

necessary material and the discipline of the entire construction yard was entrusted to the army. The king established a school here, which then became famous as the School of Mafra, directed by the Italian sculptor Alessandro Giusti, in which the techniques and art of sculpture were taught. One of the most famous of the many Portuguese artists who were trained here was Joaquim Machado de Castro. A few more statistics. The park behind the palace had a perimeter of twenty kilometers and included a hunting reserve and was the theater for banquets, entertainment and dances in the presence of the king after a hunt. The park is called *Tapada de Mafra* and should not be missed. You are likely to meet up with boars, hares, deer and hoopoe birds.

The *Mosteiro-Palácio* was the summer residence of the Portuguese sovereigns for only a few years, and now that all the religious have left the monastery, it is still partly inhabited by the army.

The rooms of the royal apartments are magnificent and furnished with exceptional pieces of 18th century furniture, splendid carpets and tapestries and collections of the finest porcelains. The walls of the *audience hall* and the *music room* are lined with 15th and 19th century paintings.

The Baroque **Basilica** is at the center of the entire

complex with two bell towers, sixty-eight meters high, each of which has fifty-seven bells, cast by Flemish foundries. Fourteen figures of saints in white Carrara marble by Italian artists of the school of Mafra grace the **narthex**. The

Palácio Nacional de Mafra - La Biblioteca

Basilica, which was not yet finished when it was consecrated, is Latin cross with a round-arch vault and a splendid **dome** over the transept crossing entirely lined in pink and white marble. The side **chapels** as well as the interior of the church are clad in marble and each chapel contains statues of saints. The most extraordinary feature of the church are the six splendid Baroque organs played on Sundays and religious holidays.

A large **cloister**, next to the Basilica, leads to the *Mosteiro* and the convent buildings. Next to the bare **cells**, the **kitchen**, the **infirmary** and the **pharmacy** still have their original furnishings and azulejos on the walls. The most amazing room is the library, eighty-five meters long, and in Rococo style. The floor is a checkerboard of red, white and black marble. The **library** contains twenty thousand books, including the precious first edition of *I Lusiadi* by Camões, the Portuguese Dante. Among the curiosities is a fascinating and rare collection of music boxes with a hundred and ten bells.

Mafra may be small, but overwhelms the visitor in its wealth and size, to be measured by statistics: a palace with nine hundred rooms, a park of many hectares, a hundred and fourteen bells, six large organs. Portugal is grandiose even in its out of the way corners.

Ericeira, a small fishing village on the coast of Prata, is located near Mafra. It is perched on the top of a rock that overlooks the ocean and is bathed in light.

White-washed houses with windows and doors painted blue and cobbled lanes surround the central square of Ericeira, the **Praça da República**. Down below the beaches with their white sand stretch out between bays and rocky reefs. It is an enchanting place, ideal for a vacation. Tourism has prospered in the last decade, above all with young people who love surfing in the waters of the beaches of **São Sebatião** with waves up to six or eight meters high. Every evening in **Porto de Pesca** one can observe the ritual of fish caught with nets and thrown on the sand, selected and salted by the fishermen before being sold. The coast is generous with lobsters, sardines and sea urchins known as *ouriços* from which the name Ericeira comes.

Why the Rooster?

Every tourist who returns from a trip to Portugal has one of the ubiquitous little roosters in his suitcase. The rooster is a symbol of Portugal. There is one in every Portuguese house or office, small or large, with a red comb or painted on an azulejo. Whatever the color, it is the official good luck symbol. The origins of this rooster symbol can be traced back to a miracle that seems to have taken place around the 15th century, when a poor pilgrim of Galicia on his way to the Shrine of Santiago de Compostotela, stopped in the city of Barcelos. The next morning the pilgrim was accused of having stolen merchandise from a land owner and was condemned to death, despite his proclamations of innocence. He was taken before the judge who was seated at table and about to eat a roast chicken. After explaining the situation, the pilgrim said that to show his innocence the roast chicken would begin crowing. Just as the poor man was being taken to the gallows, the rooster stood up and began to crow. Thanks to that rooster the pilgrim's life was saved and he could continue on his way to Compostela. In gratitude, years later the Galician returned and carved a small rooster which is supposedly the one now in the **Museu Arqueológico of Barcelos**.

What to buy

De rigueur is an azulejo tile with the characteristic brightly colored rooster, the ubiquitous good luck symbol of Portugal. Once that has been tucked in your suitcase, you can start thinking of buying something more original, typical products of the country.

While you might want to keep your eye out for the special arts and craft shops (Artesanatos) of every region, and while fine local products can also be found in the lively markets and fairs, especially away from the center, most fun can be had discovering something special. Portugal, with its old craft traditions, has a variety of really fine objects which may also be relatively inexpensive.

Let's begin with the more costly objects. Jewelery in gold and silver filigree, finely worked and original, is characteristic of the region of Porto. The Arraiolos carpets, completely handmade, in their subtle colors and motifs continue the tradition which furnished the Portuguese houses and palaces. Leather is found just about everywhere and is generally of good quality. The Algarve is particularly renowned. Other typical products of the great Portuguese

tradition are the laces and embroidered textiles, such as table cloths and bedspreads. Particularly famous is the pillow lace from Vila do Conde.

Portuguese ceramics are also lovely and original, and can be found more or less everywhere at varying prices, from simple pitchers to the black casseroles typ-

ical of some regions, to more artistic pieces for the home. The stupendous azulejos (see box), the most famous art and craft patrimony of the past and present in Portugal, must be included here. Azulejos factories can also be found in Lisbon and in the Algarve. It is difficult to resist taking home one of these lovely and truly Portuguese souvenirs. Lastly, the ephemeral and gastronomy also propose excellent products. You'll have to try the great variety of exquisite canned tuna fish, famous all over the world no less than the tasty sardine pates.

These and other foods must be accompanied by a few bottles of Porto, the most famous Portuguese wine in the world, or the cherry brandy, known as ginginha, and famous in Lisbon. An excellent solution is to buy wines and liquors in one of the many well furnished cellars to be found in every city. Lastly, no one can leave this splendid and melancholy land without taking away at least one record or cassette of its most original music, the famous fado (see box), that yearning remembrance of the sea and the soul of the Lisboetas.

ÓBIDOS

Panorama of the old town of Óbidos

Five thousand inhabitants live in one of the most historical sites n Portugal, the small and ancient Óbidos (a hundred kilometers from Lisbon), a picturesque town, over which a fort and a citadel which recall a medieval hamlet, keep watch. The impression given the visitor is almost that of an open air museum.

Once right on the ocean, it was a strategic trading center. But the sea gradually retreated, and what was once a harbor is now a laguna and fields.

The fascinating ocean walk, ten kilometers long, and a laguna with crystal clear water famous for its eels, remain almost as sentinels of the past. The tasty dishes made with eels fished here and cooked together with clams and the famous stew with laguna fish are not the only attraction Óbidos has for the many tourists and visitors. The citadel in Moorish style has been skillfully restored and is girded by a circle of crenellated walls thirteen meters high interspersed with towers and entrance gates.

The town itself is quite gay with its whitewashed houses with blue and yellow borders, flowering balconies and lace curtains at the windows. The gardens overflow with bouganvillea ranging in color from red to fuchsia. The cobbled streets and lanes wind up and down with an occasional Baroque patrician house and picturesque corners with decorated fountains. Cars are strictly prohibited.

The place is so old that as far back as 1282 Queen Isabel, wife of the poet king Dom Dinis fell in love with it and received it as a gift from her husband. From then up to 1833 Óbidos remained an appanage of the Portuguese queens.

Óbidos is a tourist town, with antique, craft and souvenir shops. Every day there is a lively well-furnished market of local products at *Porta da Vila*. Along the street, the women - mostly the older ones - crochet and work at the lace pillow, selling their beautiful laces for a few escudos at im-

The Castle of Óbidos on high over the citadel;
below: the sixteenth-century aqueduct

provised stands. Every year, on August 20th the Municipality honors and rewards the tourists free offers of grilled *sardinhas* and good red wine.

The **Castle**, now an elegant pousada (hotel), overlooks Óbidos from on high. It dates to the 13th century while the walls and towers date to the later Arab conquest.

Descending from the Castle towards **Praça de Santa Maria**, the main square of Óbidos, one encounters the *Pelourinho*, the Gothic column dating to the 15th century where rebellious servants and thieves were bound and whipped. The **Church of Santa Maria** rises up majestic on the square. Inside, next to the altar, is the Renaissance marble tomb of the governor *João de Noronha* and on the other a splendid 15th century painting by Josefa de Óbidos, a rare example of a woman painter in the story of Portuguese art.

Next to the church is the **Municipal Museum** with a collection of sacred art and French and English arms from the Napoleonic period. There is also a fine painting by the painter mentioned above, Josefa d'Óbidos (de Ayala), who was Spanish by birth and lived in a convent in Óbidos. On leaving the town be sure to visit the **Church of Senhor Jesus da Pedra** nearby. This interesting Baroque church has a splendid Early Christian stone cross on the altar.

The Church of Santa Maria on the square of the same name and the pelourinho, the Gothic fifteenth-century column; below, from the left: detail of the interior of the Church of Santa Maria, and Saint John the Baptist, polychrome sculpture of the school of Coimbra (15th cent.), in the Municipal Museum

Cuisine

Fish, above all dried, salted cod and sardines, is the principle ingredient of the joyfully humble Portuguese cuisine. It is a cuisine of the earth and of the sea, and every region has its own dish, its specialty. Everything is mixed here, and spices are used in sweet and salted dishes. Fish is cooked together with meat, sweet potatoes are accompanied with other vegetables and the result is truly tasty, and the Portuguese, proud of their batatas, are sure they are the best in the world. The ancient Romans introduced onions, garlic, wheat and wine, and as early as the 2nd century AD excellent wine was produced. The Moors and Africans brought in exotic fruits, oranges, apricots, figs, and showed the people how to dry them, as well as introducing spices such those used in curry (karil) and coriander, frequently used for its color and strong flavor. Typical of Portugal is the Sopa á Alentejana, a humble tasty soup, prepared with hot water, toasted stale bread with a poached egg and an abundant sprinkling of coriander. Another indispensable spice in the Lusitanian cuisine is cinnamon which gives both sweets and salted dishes a refined aroma. Vasco da Gama in his effort to get a monopoly on cinnamon conquered and subjected the distant land of Sri Lanka in early 16th century.

Sweets preapred with cinnamon are exquisite, such as the queijadas, tarts of short pastry and cheese, but the pastéis de nata or those of Belém are even more enticing, the former filled with cinnamon creme, the latter with vanilla cream.

In Lisbon the historical pastry shops (pastelarias) such as **Suiça**, and the **Confeitaria de Belém**, are institutions for the Lisboetas famous for their sweet tooth. Their sweets follow old 16th century from the convents. As for the excellent and well known crème caramel, it is not at all, as generally believed, a French dessert, but is Portuguese and originally from Lisbon where it is called caramelo leite creme.

Bacalhau and sardinhas, as previously mentioned, are the national dishes. The sardinhas are cooked in many ways, as well as eaten raw, fresh from the net. There are even three hundred sixty five recipes for bacalhau, the pride of Portugal, one for each day of the year. Around 1500 the Portuguese sailors caught cod in the waters of Newfoundland, the peninsula they had just conquered. The Portuguese learned how to salt it and dry it in the sun to preserve it during their long journeys.

All the restaurants, have their bacalhau dishes: boiled (cozida) with vegetables, baked or au gratin with black olives, capers, anchovies and bread crumbs. The best known is the tasty Bacalhao na Cataplana, a one dish meal, very nourishing, cooked in the typical Algarve copper pot. First onion is sautéed in butter and milk, placed on a layer of cod and fried potatoes, and then the entire dish is covered with beaten egg.

But no one must leave Lisbon or Portugal without having tried one of the tastiest dishes: the arroz de marisco, a rice dish with lots of shellfish and crustaceans flavored with mint leaves and a pinch of coriander.

Meat is important in Portugal too, cooked by itself or mixed with fish, and always accompanied by vegetables. Two decidedly appetizing specialties are lombo de porco á Alentejana, pork loin and clams in a chili pepper, garlic and oil sauce, and the frango na Pucara, chicken cooked in a clay pot. The Lusitanians, perhaps a sign of their oriental traditions, love to eat and drink at all hours of the day and night, so that the eateries, from the prestigious restaurants up to the venders who roast fish on the street, are open much longer than elsewhere.

FÁTIMA

The Roman Catholic shrine of Fátima is the largest in Western Europe, and every year four million pilgrims come here to pray, ask for grace or implore a miracle from the **Madonna of the Rosary**.

Pilgrims arrive here from all corners of the world, and the devotion is tangible, above all when the Virgin Mary is hailed at the end of the mass which concludes the pilgrimage, when the pilgrims sing and wave torches and white handkerchiefs. It is a particularly moving and awesome moment.

On May 13, 1917, the Virgin is said to have appeared for the first time to three children, the shepherds Jacinta and

The great esplanade in front of the Basilica. A few faithful are crossing it on their knees in sign of devotion

Francisco Marto nine and seven years old, and their cousin Lucia de Jesus who was ten, at **Cova de Iria**, a kilometer from Fátima. The Virgin, holding a rosary, spoke to Lucia, saying that God had been offended and inviting the children to pray for peace in the world and for communist Russia. The little shepherds were to come there for five consecutive times on the 13th of the month. Cova de Iria, a hill with holm-oaks, oaks, century-old olive trees and green pastures, suddenly became a holy appointment as people waited for the Virgin to keep faith with her promise.

On October 13th, 1917, the seventy thousand persons who had gathered under the pouring rain declared deeply moved that they had witnessed the "miracle of the sun", which was fiery red and began to rotate like a sphere. Various inexplicable healings followed.

On that occasion the Virgin revealed to Lucia, the only one with whom she spoke, a secret which was made public by the Church during the Jubilee Year 2000.

The cult of the Madonna do Rosario of Fátima, was recognized by the church in 1930. Two popes visited the site four times to pray. Paul VI went in 1967, on the 50th anniversary of the apparitions, while Pope John Paul II, visited the shrine in 1982, in 1991 and during the Holy Year.

On the site of the apparitions, near the holm oak where the shepherds saw the Angel and the Virgin for the first time, stands the **Capela das Aparições**, or Chapel of the Apparitions, rebuilt after being destroyed by a bomb attack. The holm oak no longer ex-

The portico of the Basilica; below: *the Madonna do Rosario of Fátima*

ists for it was carried away as relics by the faithful.

The **Basilica**, built in 1928, is imposing and enormous, with a tower sixty-five meters high and a large statue of the *Virgin Mary* in a niche. On top is a large crystal cross lit up during night services.

The great esplanade stretches out in front of the Basilica. Throughout the year, but especially from May 13th to October 13th, a crowd of faithful from all over the world gather here. The most fervid cross it kneeling, some crawling on the ground. For the multitudes who in the evening raise a host of torches, the site is transformed into an evocative "ocean of light".

Nearby is the **Wax Museum** that commemorates the apparitions of the Virgin of the Rosary. The walls of the Shrine are now blackened by the smoke from the infinite numbers of candles that are constantly lit, a sign of hope, accompanied by prayer. Countless *ex votos*, parts of the body reproduced in wax, mostly arms, feet, heads, legs or figures of children, have been brought here by the faithful whose prayers have been granted, in sign of thanks. Side by side with the more intimate signs of the faith, is the prosperous business of reproductions, statues and other symbols which generally go with the great pilgrimage sites.

In 1917 eight hundred people lived in Fátima. Now there are six thousand inhabitants. The two shepherds Jacinta and Francisco who died young in 1920 in the flu epidemic are buried inside the Shrine. For the Holy Year of 2000 Jacinta and Francisco have been proclaimed Blessed. Lucia de Jesus, the third shepherd who is now over ninety, has been living as a cloistered sister in the convent of Santa Dorotea in Coimbra ever since 1928.